# Yorkshire Dales

## Southern & Western Area

Dalesman Publishing Company
The Water Mill, Broughton Hall,
Skipton, North Yorkshire BD23 3AG

First Edition 1999
Reprinted 2005

Text © Terry Marsh 1999
Maps by Jeremy Ashcroft
Cover photograph: Watlowes by Simon Warner

A British Library Cataloguing-in-Publication
record is available for this book

ISBN 185568 133 1

Printed in China

# Yorkshire Dales

## Southern & Western Area

### Terry Marsh

**Companion volume to
Yorkshire Dales Northern & Eastern**

Series editor Terry Marsh

## Dalesman

# The Yorkshire Dales: S & W

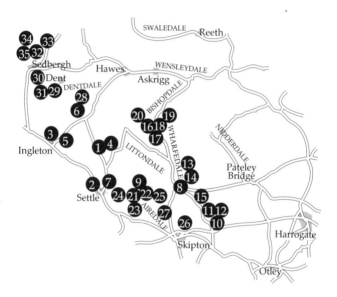

# Contents

## Airedale and Malhamdale

## Dentdale and the Howgills

# INTRODUCTION

The Yorkshire Dales possess some of the most beautiful landscapes in Britain. They attract millions of visitors each year, for tourism and recreation, for study and for work. But there are already thousands of people here, 18,000 to be more precise, a viable community of residents who live and work within the boundaries of the national park. But while tourism is becoming increasingly important, the local economy is still dependent on farming.

This is a landscape of almost infinite variety, from wild mountain uplands to verdant riverside meadows, from vast expanses of limestone pavement to equally vast expanses of peat bog, from windswept summits to the hidden depths of subterranean passages. It is a landscape that attracts people from all backgrounds and for many differing reasons, whether it is simply to appreciate the scenery or to look more deeply into the history of the region, whether it is to pass by in a carefree way or to pause and study what lies beneath our feet and all around.

And the great range of possibilities is made all the easier by a penetrating network of roads and an even more extensive mantle of footpaths and bridleways, more than a thousand miles in total, that sits neatly on top of everything. Indeed, some of Britain's finest walking routes pass through the Dales: the Pennine Way cuts south to north; the Dales Way, from Ilkley through Wharfedale, across to Dentdale and into Lakeland; the Ribble Way begins life at Ribblehead and heads south to Settle before finally quitting Dales country, and the Northern Coast to Coast Walk flits happily across the northern part, for the most part taking an intimate look at delectable Swaledale.

Between this and the companion volume, I have drawn together seventy walks, some circular, some linear, but all guiding you into a closer acquaintance with the Dales, for there is no better way to see the Dales than on foot. Walking in the Dales provides endless delight, whatever the time of year, whatever the weather.

This volume takes you into the South and West, through Ribblesdale, Wharfedale, Airedale and Malhamdale, Dentdale and the Howgills. The other covers the North and East — Swaledale, Wensleydale and Nidderdale.

It could be argued that Nidderdale is not part of the Yorkshire Dales National Park, which is true. But it is an Area of Outstanding Natural Beauty, and I prefer to think of its exclusion from the national park as a sad oversight on the part of some former bureaucrat, and an omission that should not be taken too seriously, so far as walking is concerned. Equally, a book on the Yorkshire Dales should not be expected to include a sizeable chunk of Cumbria. But this does, because although Dentdale and the Howgills are administratively within Cumbria, they are unquestionably the westerly introduction to the Dales.

All that this tells us is that it is impossible to constrain by artificial boundaries a region that is more a sense of place than somewhere you can delineate on a map. The Dales don't cease to be the Dales simply because the area you are going into is managed by a different body of people; nor is the south side of Carlin Gill in the Howgills in any significant way different from the northern side, except the former is in the national park, the latter isn't.

Daft, isn't it?

## Access by road

The Dales can be approached by road from all directions. From the north, from Kirkby Stephen, you can cut across into Birk Dale to Keld and upper Swaledale or strike south through the delectable Vale of Eden to Garsdale Head, Hawes and Wensleydale. From the south you head up from Skipton into Malhamdale, across to Settle and Ribblesdale or up to Grassington and Wharfedale. From the west you enter Dales country at Sedbergh, turning a blind eye to the fact that you're in Cumbria as you head across to Garsdale or Dentdale. From the east you come in from Richmond, Leyburn or Ripon.

## Access by public transport

Sadly, the Yorkshire Dales are not as well served by public transport as they might be.

Rail: You can get around the fringes of the Dales easily enough, but there is little scope for getting right into them. The Leeds-Settle-Carlisle railway line provides one obvious, and very attractive way, and, at Settle, this connects with services from the west.

For information specifically about trains ring 0113 224 8133 (Leeds), 01228 44711 (Carlisle), or 0345 484950 (National rail enquiries).

Bus: By bus there is a slightly better service, and most of the dales can be accessed this way. Some however, Malham for example, have very limited services, often only once or twice a day and during summer months only. Bus services are changing all the time, however, so it is always wisest to obtain up-to-date information from the appropriate tourist information centre (see below) before committing yourself to using public transport.

Some areas also have a postbus service — Wensleydale, for example — and this can be a useful, inexpensive and interesting way of getting about.

## Accommodation

The Yorkshire Dales has a wide selection of accommodation — hotels, guest houses, B&Bs, self-catering and youth hostels. Expect many places to be fully booked during the main tourist seasons, but if you are prepared to go during autumn and the winter months, you will find numerous places that are inexpensive and welcoming.

# Equipment

All walkers have their own preferences in the matter of equipment and clothing, but the following list may be found a useful reminder — rucksack (comfortable, well padded), boots, socks, trousers (or shorts, etc., but not shorts alone — at certain times of the year there are a lot of nettles), underclothes, shirt, midwear (e.g. pullover) and spare, wind- and waterproof jacket and overtrousers, hat, gloves, maps, compass, torch (with spare battery and bulbs), whistle, first aid kit, survival bag or space blanket, food and drink, and (if necessary) insect repellent.

Do not be lulled into thinking that the proximity of villages from which help can be obtained means that you do not need to carry essential equipment. Even the shortest, simplest walks can become a severe test of patience and endurance if someone is injured and has to be left on the fells while help is brought.

## Maps

The walks in this volume are covered on the following Ordnance Survey Outdoor Leisure Maps:

| | | |
|---|---|---|
| 2 | — | Yorkshire Dales: Southern and Western area |
| 19 | — | Howgill Fells |
| 30 | — | Yorkshire Dales: Northern and Central areas |

# Information

**Yorkshire Dales National Park Information Service**, Colvend, Hebden Road, Grassington, Skipton, North Yorkshire BD23 5LB (Tel. 01756 752748). You can also try their web site on http://www.yorkshirenet.co.uk/visinfo/ydales

## National Park Centres

Aysgarth Falls (01969 663424)

Clapham (015242 51419)

Grassington (01756 752774)

Hawes (01969 667450)

Malham (01729 830363)

Sedbergh (015396 20125

**Yorkshire Tourist Board**, 312 Tadcaster Road, York YO2 2HF (Tel. 01904 707961). You can also visit their web site on http://www.ytb.org.uk

## Tourist Information Centres

Horton-in-Ribblesdale (01729 860333)

Ingleton (015242 41049)

Leyburn (01969 623069)

Pateley Bridge (01423 711147)

Reeth (01748 884059)

Richmond (01748 850252)

Settle (01729 825192)

Skipton (01756 792809)

# RIBBLESDALE

Ribblesdale probably isn't the foremost dale of the Yorkshire Dales that people think of; in some ways the close association of the Ribble with Lancashire and the Ribble Estuary at Preston tends to give it a Red Rose rather than White Rose feel. But there is no denying that the river rises high in Three Peak country and doesn't in fact reach Lancashire until it approaches Gisburn, and even there it's a part of modern Lancashire that was pinched from Yorkshire. This westwards tendency is also underlined by the fact that while most of the Yorkshire Dales per se send their waters flowing eastwards to the North Sea, Ribblesdale, lying west of the Pennine watershed, flows west into the Irish Sea.

The main part of the dale with which this book is concerned is principally the stretch from Whernside and Ribblehead down as far as Settle. Between the bleakness of Ribblehead, with its spectacular viaduct, and the bustle of Settle there are no towns and only one sizeable village, Horton.

One of the key focal points for walking in the Dales, Horton-in-Ribblesdale is a straggly collection of 17th- and 18th-century grey stone houses and cottages in the shadow of Pen-y-ghent. The village is old enough to be mentioned in the Domesday Book, and it was here that Henry VI came during the Wars of the Roses (1455-87) to evade his enemies. The sturdy church of St Oswald at the southern end of the village has a good deal of Norman masonry, and a few medieval fragments of stained glass in the west window. Like a number of villages in the Dales, Horton had its school in the churchyard.

Through the dale's length runs the famous Settle to Carlisle railway line, which, condemned to extinction, was saved only by a massive campaign that resulted in a last minute reprieve. To see the number of people using it today makes you wonder how anyone could have contemplated closing it in the first place; but that's sentimental-speak, not the economics of business.

Beautiful as it is, there remains an austere feel about Ribblesdale that isn't present in any of the other dales, except Nidderdale. The absence of substantial stands of trees, long since gone to fire lime kilns, has something to do with it, and the way the farmsteads seem to have pushed just so far northwards up the valley, getting higher and higher, before giving up and letting Nature take over. Everywhere is farmed, of course, but the further north you go the more bleak is the setting, the less likely you are to see tamed, green pastures.

The area has been inhabited since the earliest times. When the Romans arrived, the dale, or more to the point the land above it, was already inhabited by the Brigantes, who built a hill-fort on the summit of Ingleborough. It was from this elevated position that the Brigantian leader, Venutius, led a revolt against the Romans which was not finally quelled until AD74, by Julius Agricola.

Later came the Angles and the Norsemen, occupying the valley sides and, where possible, the river valleys so that by the time of the Norman conquest, this part of the country, like much of the dales, was well settled. That Ribblesdale continued to be an important place is evidenced by the many old packhorse tracks that flow out in all directions. Some are based on Roman foundations, while other more recent routes lead to Malhamdale and Wharfedale and to Dentdale. Most of these developed during the time the area was occupied and farmed by the great monastic abbeys of Fountains, Sawley, Bolton and others.

Many of these ancient tracks can still be traced on maps, though in places less obviously on the ground. Yet along them for well over a hundred years went the packhorse trains of galloway ponies, up to twenty animals in single file with a man at the head and a boy bringing up the rear.

Today a modern highway visits the dale, the Pennine Way, which creeps in over the top of Pen-y-ghent, and slinks out northwards, along the course of a Roman road, Cam High Road, bound for Bainbridge.

At the southern end of the dale, Settle has existed since at least Saxon times. It has a market charter going back to the 13th century, and still has a delightful 'old world' feel about it — but not quite that old!

# 1 Selside and Sulber

*To the west of Horton runs the famous Settle-Carlisle railway line, and, because the village centre car park is invariably full from the beginning of spring, this walk, which samples both sides of the valley, begins from the station in the hope of encouraging walkers to leave their cars at home, and enjoy a leisurely approach by train. The line is linked to many towns throughout the North West, and trains run at times that leave ample time to complete the walk, and, perhaps, have a snack in the Pen-y-ghent Cafe, before returning home.*

**Distance:** *8 miles/13km* *tracks throughout*
**Height gain**: *950ft/290m* **Start/Finish:** *Horton-in-*
**Walking time:** *4 hours* *Ribblesdale station*
**Type of walk:** *Good* *GR804726*

From the station go forward towards the centre of Horton, about a quarter of a mile away, and after crossing the Ribble bridge ignore the first road on the left and, taking great care against approaching traffic at what is a difficult bend, go a few strides further to the Crown Inn. Turn left to pass in front of the pub to join the northbound Pennine Way, a rough-surfaced track between walls.

*The name of the pub signifies a loyalty to the reigning monarch at the time the pub was built. There are more*

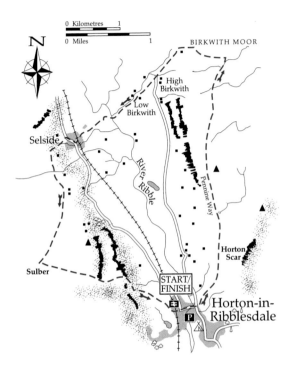

than 500 'Crown Inns' in England, though many of them disappeared during Cromwell's time, only to reappear following the Restoration.

Along the first part of the walled lane, Pen-y-ghent is dramatically in view on the right, before disappearing behind grassy hillocks. There is, too, a fine retrospective view to Horton and down the Ribblesdale valley, and as *the track rises so the view opens up of Ingleborough across the valley, and the squat mound of Whernside, the highest of Yorkshire's 'Three Peaks' to the north-west.*

Keep going up the Pennine Way, for about 3 miles/5km, gaining height gradually, to reach Birkwith Moor at a gate, where the Pennine Way is signposted to the left. Go left along a gently rising track, continuing now towards Ling Gill Bridge.

The Pennine Way soon comes down to cross a wall by a stile beside an isolated barn. Over the stile go forward alongside a wall on your left. The path becomes a rough track. Stay on this to meet a broad access track. Go left, and on through a gate, then down to a metal gate on the left, now leaving the Pennine Way.

Beyond the gate, go down past the entrance to Old Ing Farm, continuing forward to descend to High Birkwith. At High Birkwith go through a gate to a surfaced lane, leaving this 40yds/m further on, over a wall at a through-stile and onto a signposted footpath for Selside.

Descend half left across the ensuing field to a ladder-stile. The path goes through a small stand of trees, and then down the next field to another ladder-stile, and then continue downfield towards Low Birkwith Farm.

As you approach the farm, go through a gate to its right, and as you pass the first building turn left into the farmyard, and then go forward through a gate (signposted to Selside). Through the gate keep forward to reach a stream, Coppy Gill. Turn left, with the stream on your right, and follow it to its confluence with the River Ribble, crossing three fields along the way.

As you approach the Ribble you cross Coppy Gill by a footbridge, and then turn to cross the Ribble on a more substantial bridge. On the other side, pass through a gate and go forward into the next field. Be guided by a fence on your left, soon to reach a gate at a wall junction. Cross a through-stile and go along a walled lane, and shortly bear right on a signposted footpath to Selside, still continuing as a walled lane.

Keep on past a farm and out along its access, a rough, stony lane that goes under the Settle-Carlisle railway line, and keep on to meet the main road in the farming hamlet of Selside. Turn right, and follow the road for 150yds/m, and then leave it, on the left, along a broad, walled track, often lined with the cars of potholers bound for Alum Pot. When you reach a gate giving access to Alum Pot, turn left on a walled lane to a ladder-stile.

Beyond the stile, go forward with a wall on your right, for about 150yds/m to a wall corner, and then branch left across a field to a ladder-stile to the left of a gate. Once more, Pen-y-ghent is in view across the moors, a splendid sight.

Continue in the same direction, slightly left, to the far side of a field, to a ladder-stile to the right of a gate. Over the stile, cross the next field, and afterwards bear right on a green track across open moorland that forms part of the Ingleborough National Nature Reserve.

The way across the moor is waymarked with small poles topped with blue paint, and the track guides you on to meet a wall and gate. About 400yds/m after crossing the wall, you reach the signpost at Sulber, where a popular track has descended from Ingleborough, and another goes forward eventually to reach the village of Clapham. Turn left at the signpost, to go down a long, clear track through the limestone outcrops of Sulber Nick to return to Horton.

# 2 Stainforth and Giggleswick Scar

*This delightful circuit, which can be started just as easily in Settle, climbs onto the limestone moors below Smearsett Scar, drops to the hamlet of Feizor, and then returns along the prominent escarpment of Giggleswick Scar, which here marks the boundary of the Yorkshire Dales National Park.*

**Distance:** *7¹/₂ miles / 12km*
**Height gain:** *885ft/270m*
**Walking time:** *4 hours*
**Type of walk:** *Generally* *on good paths, but potentially confusing in mist*

**Start/Finish:** *Stainforth car park. GR821673*

Leave the car park along a footpath beside Stainforth Beck that leads beneath the main road to a picnic area. Turn right and walk up to the road, turning left towards Horton. After about 200yds/m turn left onto a side road that crosses the railway and descends to meet the River Ribble at Stainforth Bridge, an attractive single-arch bridge dating from 1675.

Cross the bridge and keep forward on a rising lane. At the top of the lane, cross a road and go forward up a surfaced farm lane. When the lane turns into a farmyard, leave it and go ahead through a gate onto a rising track. When this forks, branch right to a ladder stile. The on-going track rises in bends before becoming more purposeful and striking out across upland pastures, initially heading in the direction of Smearsett Scar. A succession of upland pastures (potentially confusing in poor visibility) and stiles ends just east of Feizor. A final ladder stile gives onto a path descending beside a wall. A sunken pathway leads down to a small gate, and crosses a small enclosure before finally reaching the village lane.

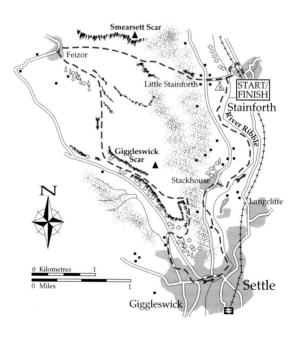

Turn left and go down the lane for 70yds/m, then leave it, on the left, on a rising track (signposted for Stackhouse) that eventually levels out to cross a broad green sward. Keep on along the path to a wall corner, and then start branching right to a signpost. When you reach it, go right and down to a ladder stile and gate. Over the stile go forward with a wall on your right. When this changes direction keep forward across moorland pasture to a ladder stile, and then bear right on a broad green path that leads across more pastures to a signpost for Giggleswick.

The continuing path descends limestone outcrops as it heads for a final stile before reaching the prominent pathway that undulates across the top of Giggleswick Scar. Keep going, as far as a quarry. Go round the perimeter fence to reach a path descending to a tall iron gate. Through the gate keep following the path down; it goes through undergrowth before finally reaching the road.

Cross the road, bearing right, and take the lane on the left, directly opposite the quarry entrance. Go down the lane and keep on until, just past the final entrance to Giggleswick School, which dates from the 16th and 17th centuries, you can go through a wall gap into Pape's Field, and along a perimeter surfaced pathway that brings you out at the rear of St Alkeda's Church.

*The church of St Alkeda is only 500 years old, but has seen many changes, while the history of a church here goes back more than 1,000 years. The church saw violent* times during the time of the Border Troubles, when it was raided by Scots, during the Wars of the Roses, and at the time of the Rising in the North. The church contains many interesting features that make it well worth a visit.

Little is known, however, about the saint, although the story that has passed down through the ages is that she was a Saxon lady murdered for her faith by a group of Danish women at the time of the Norman conquest.

Go round the church to pass in front of it, and then keep on to a road junction, keeping right into Bankwell Road. Leave the road after a bend, along a surfaced ginnel between two large houses. This leads to the River Ribble, meeting it at Giggleswick Memorial Bridge, which can be used to visit Settle.

Keep on past the bridge on a surfaced path to a gap stile. The river along this stretch is well populated with bird life, notably dipper, grey wagtail, kingfisher and goosander.

When the path rises to meet the main road, cross it and go down a pathway opposite between a wall and fence. Follow this round the end of a playing field, and then through a wall gap stile, before striking out across a field to a gated gap stile on the far side. Beyond, follow a wall then a fence along the top of a raised embankment above the river. At another gap stile, go forward across a field to reach a lane.

At the lane turn right and when it forks, branch right, and a short way further on leave the lane and turn right (signposted for The Locks). This leads back to the Ribble. Turn left over a through stile onto a grassy riverside path. The path wanders on, never far from the river, crossing numerous fields and stiles either on low-lying pasture or on raised embankments.

Finally it brings you to the spectacle of Stainforth Force, a series of fine, low waterfalls that are especially splendid when in spate. Beyond these you reach Stainforth Bridge once more, from which you simply retrace your steps to the car park.

# 3 The Ingleton Glens

*It must come as something of a surprise to find that there is actually one walk at least in the Dales that gets better when it rains. But that is true of this walk, commonly known as 'The Waterfalls Walk', and immensely popular on that account alone. In view of this popularity, it is usually better either to do the walk early in the day (while most visitors are still tackling breakfast) or during the winter months. There is, however, a charge for admission to the main part of the walk.*

**Distance:** *4 miles/6.5km*
**Height gain:** *540ft/165m*
**Walking time:** *2½-3 hours*
**Type of walk:** *Easy*

*walking on good paths; numerous steps*
**Start/Finish:** *Ingleton car park. GR695730*

*At Ingleton the rivers Twiss and Doe combine to become the River Greta, but before they do they each produce a fine series of waterfalls. This walk visits all of them. But, in addition to being so popular for its scenery, the walk follows a geological itinerary of great importance. It involves crossing three major fault lines, several dykes, magnificent outcrops, and a splendid example of what the geologists call an 'unconformity'.*

*Ingleton, too, is not without its share of interest. It is renowned as the heart of Dales limestone country, and is dominated by a defunct railway viaduct built in 1859.*

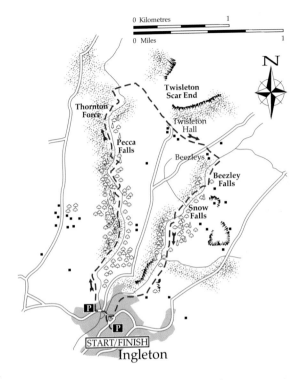

*The church of St Mary has a Perpendicular west tower, though the rest is Victorian.*

From the village car park turn right and then left to go down to cross the two rivers just above their confluence, and then turn right into the car park at the base of the Waterfalls Walk, which is where you'll need to pay your admission fee. The car park is built on debris washed down by the torrent that

27

cut the valley south of Thornton Force. As the valley widened, so the river slackened off and deposited much of the water-borne material.

The route heads up into Swilla Glen, a tree-flanked gorge, and eventually crosses the river at Manor Bridge. Here can be seen the first indication of the North Craven Fault in the form of sandy-coloured limestone outcropping immediately above the bluish calcareous mudstone seen at stream level. Higher up you recross the river at Pecca Bridge, just before which, on the opposite bank, another fault has placed the mudstone against Ingleton slates. The nearby quarry also provides some interesting features for geologists, especially in providing a contrast between bedding and cleavage.

The path continues upstream past the Pecca Falls, where there are fine outcrops of green greywacke sandstone interbedded with slate. The ascending path finally leaves the trees as it passes Constitution Hill, and continues past Cuckoo Island.

At a sharp right bend you get your first glimpse of Thornton Force, one of the most famous geological localities in Britain. Here water plummets over a notch in Lower Carboniferous limestone into a pool. The limestone overhangs the lower part of the fall; the upper is limestone, the lower Ingleton slates. The junction between the two is marked by a ledge that represents an ancient beach on a wave-cut platform near a sea cliff.

Continue up the rocky path to the left of the fall, which wanders round the terminal moraine of Raven Ray which blocked off the southern end of Kingsdale, and caused the post-glacial diversion of the stream. Nearby, cross Raven Ray Bridge and walk up-field to Twistleton Lane and Twistleton Hall. Go down past this farm to meet Oddie's Lane. Cross the lane and go down to Beezleys Farm, passing between the buildings to a gate on the left.

Branch left to go to Beezley Falls to complete the glens walk in the company of the River Doe. The falls along the way — Beezley, Snow and Cat's Leap — are not as spectacular as those of the Twiss, but they are attractive nonetheless. By continuing alongside the river you eventually return to the centre of Ingleton, from where the car park is easily reached.

# 4 Pen-y-ghent and Plover Hill

*Pen-y-ghent is altogether too irresistible a summit to ignore; its profile, especially when viewed from Horton, is magnificent. Most ascents, however, make use of the Pennine Way, and few walkers bother to continue northwards to visit Plover Hill and the delightful old Foxup Road to the north.*

**Distance:** *7½ miles /12km*
**Height gain:** *1,705ft /520m*
**Walking time:** *4-5 hours*
**Type of walk:** *A high* *level, invigorating walk mainly on good paths, some boggy*
**Start/Finish:** *Horton-in-Ribblesdale GR807726*

Walk down the Settle road and go past Horton church (St Oswald's) and take the second turning on the left.

*St Oswald's Church is both rugged and ancient, and boasts a complete Norman nave, which is unique in this part of the country. Although it comes early in the walk, it is worth taking a few minutes to visit, for it contains a Norman font, some interesting fragments of early glass and a number of mason's marks.*

Keep following the surfaced lane round, and at the

first farm on the left, leave it on a signposted track for Pen-y-ghent, crossing a stile and bearing left beside a wall. This leads to a through stile at a wall corner, now with Pen-y-ghent fully in view ahead.

Keep on in the same direction over a succession of walls and stiles on a resurfaced path. Eventually the path leads to a double stile on the ridge wall, below the prow of Pen-y-ghent. Over the stiles turn left and follow the path up onto Pen-y-ghent, which goes up in two distinct steps. The lower part, on limestone, can be slippery when wet. The upper part is formed into an elongated staircase, and leads to the edge of the sloping summit plateau from which a graded path runs on to the highest point.

Cross the ridge-wall stile, and turn right, walking beside the wall on a footpath signposted to Foxup. Keep following the wall, cross an intermediate wall, and continue to a wall junction on the edge of Plover Hill; the highest point, marked by a large cairn, cannot be reached by right of way. Cross another stile, turn left and walk away from the wall across open moorland (signposted: Foxup Road).

After starting to descend at an easy angle the path then goes down more steeply as it deals with the escarpment edge, and then relaxes the gradient a little as it drops to meet Foxup Road. The path brings you down beside a wall to a gate. Here turn left on a signposted footpath for Horton-in-Ribblesdale.

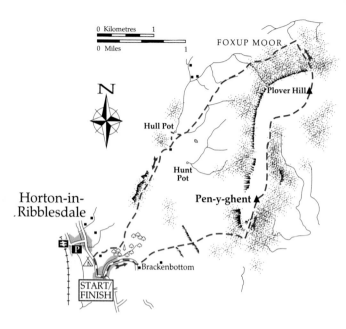

The path continues, never far from a wall, across the intermittently boggy expanse of Horton Moor, crossing numerous streams on the way to reach a gate. As you follow the track down across the moor you meet another track at right angles. This is not a right of way, so continue on the original track which curves round to a ladder stile just to the east of Hull Pot, to which a diversion is easily made. The concluding stage of the walk then runs on down to meet the Pennine Way at the end of the walled lane from Horton, and follows this back to the village.

# 5 Ingleborough and Sulber

*Viewed from the south-west, Ingleborough rises as an isolated summit from an extensive plateau of limestone culminating in a fine series of scars overlooking Chapel-le-Dale. Once thought to have been the highest summit in England, the mountain has unique appeal.*

| | |
|---|---|
| **Distance:** 10½ miles/17km | **Type of walk:** *A fine walk of no great difficulty* |
| **Height gain:** 1,840ft/560m | **Start/Finish:** *National Park car park and information centre, Clapham. GR746692* |
| **Walking time:** 5-6 hours | |

*Clapham, where this walk begins, is a village of considerable delight, a place of old bridges and waterfalls, white cottages, old stone houses and stands of ancient trees. Not far away the great sprawl of Ingleborough dominates the countryside of west Craven, its distinctive flat-topped summit a feature easily identifiable from as far away as the Lakeland Fells.*

The walk starts with a pleasant passage alongside Clapham Beck, having left the car park, near the National Park Information Centre, and turns right to cross the beck by an old stone bridge. A variety of attractive cottages leads to the fine church of St James, largely rebuilt in 1814, though its fine

33

Perpendicular tower dates from the 14th century.

Continue past the entrance to the grounds of Ingleborough Hall Estate to follow Clapdale Lane (signposted: Ingleborough; Gaping Gill; Ingleborough Cave) and keep on as far as Clapdale Farm where a sharp descent, right, back towards the beck, reunites you with the path from the estate grounds.

*Ingleborough Hall, now an outdoor centre, was formerly the home of Reginald Farrer (1880-1920), a renowned botanist who during the second half of his brief life made repeated journeys to far corners of the world in pursuit of his passion, and brought many foreign plant specimens to Clapham to decorate the grounds of the Farrer estate.*

Further along Clapham Beck you pass Ingleborough Cave to continue through a sheltered glen between low scars of limestone.

*In the early years of the 19th century the underground network of caverns between Gaping Gill and Clapham Beck Head remained a source of mystery and wonder. Ingleborough Cave, the obvious entrance, was blocked after only a short distance, although floods suggested that this cave might be connected to the underground river of Gaping Gill. So, in 1837, the landowner ordered the blockage to be broken down, to drain away the lake it held back, and to enable exploration of the interior. A fine cavern was found part of the way to Gaping Gill, but it took almost another 150 years of exploration before the final connection was made.*

Ahead the main valley curves to the left and a stile helps you into the rocky ravine of Trow Gill. Rising steadily the gorge is overlooked by slopes both higher and steeper. The gorge narrows dramatically to a spill of boulders over which you must clamber to reach the dry, grassy valley beyond.

*Trow Gill is a classic example of a limestone gorge, fashioned by a surface stream of meltwater flowing off the limestone plateau above as the glaciers retreated at the end of the last Ice Age.*

The path here follows the line of a wall to a couple of adjacent stiles, beyond which lies the broad limestone plateau of Ingleborough. Only a few strides ahead, on the left, a sizeable pothole, Bar Pot, provides cavers (and cavers only!) with the easiest access into the Gaping Gill system whose network of caverns underlies all this stretch of moorland.

Ahead rise the broad slopes of Little Ingleborough, with the main summit rising beyond. The onward route is obvious, picking a way around the worst stretches of bog to begin the ascent to the first minor summit.

*Away to the right, however, surrounded by a fence, lies the most famous of all potholes, Gaping Gill. The pot takes its name from its great entrance, which swallows with ease the waters of Fell Beck as they gather from the high grounds of Ingleborough. This wide open hole, of obviously great depth, was an irresistible challenge to the explorers of the 19th century, but it was not until*

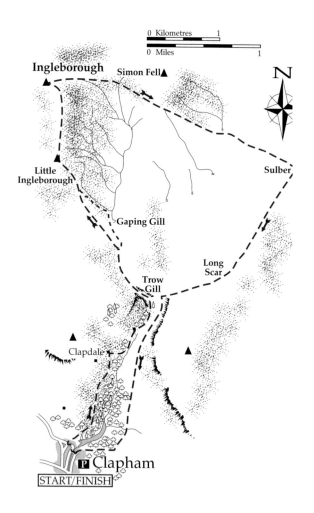

Inglebrough

Simon Fell▲

N

Little
Inglebrough

Gaping Gill

Sulber

Long
Scar

Trow
Gill

Clapdale

▲ Clapham

START/FINISH

0 Kilometres 1

0 Miles 1

36

*the last decade of the century that a Frenchman, Edouard Martel, in August 1895, finally reached the floor of the shaft. The main chamber of Gaping Gill is the largest cavern in Britain, 140yds/m long and almost 30yds/m high and wide.*

From Gaping Gill the path heads north-west for the base of Little Ingleborough which is gained by a steepish pull to a collection of shelter-cairns on its upper edge from where there is a fine view across Ribblesdale to Pen-y-ghent and Fountains Fell. A path now leads onwards across marshy ground to begin a slanting ascent to the rim of Ingleborough's main summit.

*As you reach the rim you pass through the remains of a hill-fort wall, a massive encircling wall, now collapsed, around the edge of a summit plateau which also contains the foundations, still traceable in the peaty summit, of nineteen circular huts believed to be a settlement of the first Iron Age man in this district.*

The continuation to the summit follows a line of small cairns to a massive cairn beside a trig point and a crossed-wall shelter surmounted by a view indicator and erected by the Ingleton Fell and Rescue Team to commemorate the Coronation of Queen Elizabeth in 1953. The highest point, the true summit, is marked by another cairn on a rocky plinth a few strides north-west of the trig, overlooking the Doe valley and the long descent to Crina Bottom and Ingleton.

The onward descent leaves the north-east corner of the summit plateau to gain a path along the southern flank of Simon Fell to a derelict shooting hut. Beyond lies a weird landscape known as Sulber Scars, a massive desert of fissured white limestone through which a path picks its way to a lonely signpost at GR778735. Horton-in-Ribblesdale lies not far ahead, but here we must turn right on a grassy path to reach a stile at Sulber Gate.

From the stile continue ahead, keeping the wall on your left, and when the path forks at a cairn a short distance further on, keep right, making for the conspicuous cairn on Long Scar. Before reaching Long Scar, however, another cairn marks a change of direction, again right, to enter a wide grassy amphitheatre known as Clapham Bottoms. The path is clear enough and brings you via one gate to another at the head of Long Lane, an old bridleway connecting Clapham and Selside in Ribblesdale.

As you go down Long Lane there are fine views across woodlands below in which shelters the village of Clapham, while a conspicuous dip in the lane marks the line of the North Craven Fault. Long Lane in due course meets Thwaites Lane at a T-junction; this ancient route is a continuation of Mastiles Lane across Malham Moor, a monastic highway that crossed the southern Dales to link the estates of Fountains Abbey.

Turn right into Thwaite Lane and descend towards Clapham, passing through two tunnels built by the Farrers to protect the privacy of their estate. This tunnelled lane ends near Clapham church at the top end of the village, from where, left, you will find the car park only a short distance away.

# 6 Whernside

*This is probably the most indirect route to the summit of Whernside, and came about because of restoration work that was being carried out on the direct ascent from Winterscales. It does give a longer walk, but it is ideal for a warm day when getting to the top is only incidental to being out walking among the hills and valleys of the Dales.*

| | |
|---|---|
| **Distance:** 7¹/₂ miles /12km | **Type of walk:** *On good paths, but exposed on the summit ridge* |
| **Height gain:** 1,510ft/460m | **Start/Finish:** *Ribblehead GR764791* |
| **Walking time:** *4-5 hours* | |

*Whernside is, as attractive mountains go, just plain ugly, a great dollop of a summit that owes its fame as much, if not more, to the fact that it is one of Yorkshire's celebrated 'Three Peaks' than to the distinction that it is the highest of the summits in the Yorkshire Dales. The mountain is a vastly elongated ridge, with a wall all along its summit, which makes it a relatively safe place to be in poor visibility — though this can still be an unnerving experience. It is, however, still a summit that every visitor to the Dales should 'bag' at some stage.*

From Ribblehead follow the broad track heading for the viaduct.

*The viaduct is indisputably a remarkable piece of engineering, and a reminder of the Midland Railway's determination to force its own route through to Scotland. It was built at enormous cost both financially and in terms of human life. For some time the railway was threatened with closure, and a vigorous campaign waged to keep it open. The campaign proved successful when, in 1989, Margaret Thatcher's Government announced that the line was to remain open.*

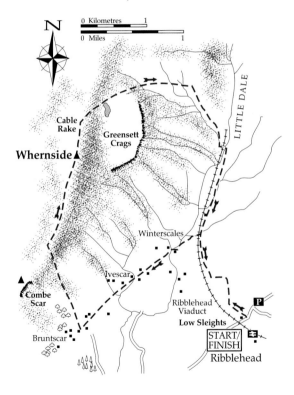

As the track bends left to go under the viaduct, leave it and go forward onto a grassy path leading to a renovated footpath. Go along this, climbing steps, and then onto a pathway. Keep going past one turning under the railway, and on to Blea Moor Sidings.

Cross a stile on the way, continuing beside a wall. About 300yds/m before the Blea Moor Signal Box and just by a railway signal, turn left to go under the railway.

On the other side, follow a rough track down to meet a stream. Go left along it towards Winterscales Farm. Cross the stream by a single arch bridge near the farm. Go forward and pass to the left of the farm on a surfaced lane.

At the next farm the surfaced lane ends. Go past the farm and descend left on a waymarked bridleway through gates and across a field to another gate. Beyond that the bridleway continues as a rough vehicle track beside a wall and fence/hedgerows. In the middle of the next field the path forks. Branch right to a gate in a wall, and go across the next field on a green path, then on across two more fields to reach another farm, continuing past that on another field track to meet the main line of ascent to Whernside from the Old Hall Inn.

Turn right to access a wide grassy pasture. A clear path now climbs the hill slope ahead, becoming steeper the closer you get to the intake wall, beyond which steps lead up the final edge to the ridge.

Only minor undulations remain between you and the summit to which you are unerringly guided by the accompanying wall. Just near the summit the wall marks the boundary between North Yorkshire and Cumbria, and the summit trig lies beyond the wall in Cumbria — though I believe there is marginally higher ground a few strides further along the wall, in Yorkshire.

The continuation to Ribblehead sets off alongside the wall, which still accompanies you along the top of the ridge. When you reach a large cairn the route descends eastwards towards Little Dale. Lower down it joins the Craven Way, an ancient track across the fells, at a stile. The valley bottom is reached near the entrance to Blea Moor Tunnel, an outstanding feat of engineering on the Settle-Carlisle railway line, burrowing under the moors for almost 1¼ miles/2km; it was constructed in the 1870s.

The bridge spanning the railway line, incidentally, is also an aqueduct carrying the waters of Force Gill.

Ahead you cross Little Dale Beck before continuing along a prominent track to Blea Moor Sidings, beyond which you rejoin your outward route.

# 7 Attermire and Victoria Cave

*Many visitors to Settle remain unaware of the out-standing landscape above this busy little market town as they head off in search of other wonders. Here, in the backyard of the town, there are caves and crags as fine as any in the Dales, and well worth this brief encounter.*

| | |
|---|---|
| **Distance:** *4¹/₂ miles/7km* | *walking on paths, tracks* |
| **Height gain:** *820ft/250m* | *and lanes* |
| **Walking time:** *3 hours* | **Start/Finish:** *Settle* |
| **Type of walk:** *Easy* | *GR820637* |

*Settle is a delightful market town largely occupying the east bank of the River Ribble, below the limestone crag of Castlebergh. It is a bustling place of narrow ginnels and steep lanes, of attractive buildings and that comfortable, friendly air that seems to deposit itself on places that have considerable antiquity. Not that everyone felt the buildings had anything of note about them: Thomas Gray, the poet, who visited Settle in 1769, wrote: "There are not in it above a dozen good-looking houses, the rest are old and low with little porticos in front."*

*The town was originally part of the properties of the Percys of Northumberland, one of whom, Henry, in 1249 was granted a market charter that was increased by additional fairs in 1708. One contemporary writer in the early 19th century described the place as "full of apple or potato carts, and of the visits of travelling companies: for instance, four large caravans with the skeleton of a whale 85 feet long, and Wombwell's menagerie 'drawn by 45 stout horses in 14 caravans'".*

Leave the centre of Settle across the market and up past the Trustee Savings Bank and the Talbot Arms Hotel and keep going, branching left as you reach The Folly. There branch right onto Victoria Street, which is signposted to Kirkby Malham and Airton. Go on up Albert Hill.

In Upper Settle, when the roadway next forks, ignore the road going off to Kirkby Malham and bear right onto a 'No Through Road'. A short way further on, branch left up a waterworks access track (signposted: Lambert Lane). At the top of the service track cross a stile and ascend, left, beside a wall above, and then turn right alongside the wall to a gap on the left. Go through this and then over a ladder stile 30yds/m away. Beyond the stile go forward beside a wall to a wall junction. Cross the wall by a through stile and keep on in the same direction to reach Lambert Lane at a gate.

Turn left up this old track to meet High Hill Lane, the surfaced road to Kirkby Malham. Turn right for 130yds/m and then branch left onto Stockdale Lane to a right-hand bend 200yds/m further on. There leave the lane, over a ladder stile, going forward on a footpath beside a wall (signposted: Attermire Scar).

On topping a slight rise the crags of Attermire Scar

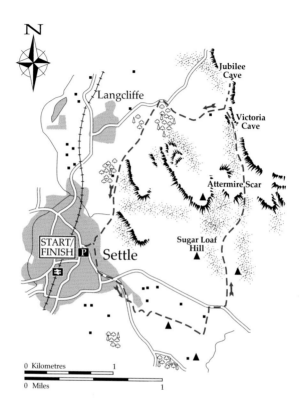

come into view ahead. The footpath has now become a broad grassy track and keeps on in the same direction to the left of Sugar Loaf Hill, and eventually passes a signpost in mid-pasture, beyond which the on-going track is occasionally waymarked to a gate.

Beyond the gate go across two walled enclosures.

Once across the intake wall, turn right on a grassy path and about 120yds/m later swing left to go up into a valley between Warrendale Knotts and Attermire Scar. Attermire Cave can be seen above the scree slopes ahead, a slim, vertical opening in the cliff face.

When a ladder stile appears on the right, cross it, and follow the on-going path below Attermire Scar in a northerly direction, heading for the conspicuous Victoria Cave. The cave was named to commemorate its discovery in the year of Queen Victoria's coronation in 1838.

*All is peaceful now, but it is clear from finds in Victoria and other caves that the countryside here was once inhabited by animals long since extinct — straight-tusked elephant, slender-nosed rhinoceros, woolly hippopotamus and ox — as well as more commonplace animals — reindeer, badger, dogs, arctic fox and sheep.*

The path beyond the stile is a broad grassy track that leads to a wall corner below Brent Scar from where parallel footpaths lead on to a ladder stile.

Having past Victoria Cave, keep on to another stile. Over this descend left to pass through a gate, but before you do, go forward a short way further to see the twin entrances to Jubilee Cave. Return to the gate, and beyond follow the on-going vehicle track, which runs on down past woodlands to meet a surfaced lane. When it does, go left, through a gate on a bridleway (signposted: Settle).

Crossing a field the bridleway descends to a gate

and continues as a narrow path below a wall and beech woodland. A clear path continues down through gates and alongside a wall, and runs on to become a walled lane. A short way on it crosses the bottom of a hill pasture, following the line of a wall, eventually to meet another walled lane, that leads down towards the centre of Settle.

When you meet a surfaced lane, go forward, and follow the descending lane (Constitution Hill) down to the right, into Settle.

# WHARFEDALE AND LITTONDALE

If you enter Wharfedale from the north, near its birthplace high on the moors above Cam Houses, never having seen the lower valley, you might contest my claim that Wharfedale is consistently lovely, with beauty at every turn. At the head of Langstrothdale there is still a tang of the wilderness that once formed part of a great hunting chase, and it is not until you descend past Beckermonds, by which time the river is beginning to flex its muscles, that you begin to realise that here might be something special.

From its source, the river flows crystal clear, gathering waters from a myriad side streams as it goes, and moving for the most part at a modest pace as it flows across slabby beds and down miniature cascades. But the river is perfectly capable of changing its demeanour in a moment. Flooded by heavy rainfall it becomes an angry, raging torrent, so that where you may have paddled your feet in the morning, by the afternoon you could be swept off them. Camden, that great historian, wrote in 1610: "Wherf runneth with a swift and speedy streame, making a great noise as hee goeth, as if he were froward, stubborne and angry." Lives have been lost in the Wharfe since the earliest times.

The underlying rocks of limestone, capped with gritstone in a few places, are a perfect element for the numerous streams. The whole landscape has been fashioned by water, either free-flowing, or frozen in the form of long-retreated glaciers. It is a canvas on which Man has placed his imprint of winding roads, mines, walls, farm buildings and the most attractive villages imaginable. Of those visited in the walks that follow Buckden is now a highly popular tourist haunt, revealing nothing of its ancient background as a focal point for the hunting activities of the nobility or of the Scandinavian influences that developed the landscape. Downriver, Starbotton is a delightful 17th-century village, while Kettlewell, another immensely popular spot, has always been a self-contained and busy settlement. Grassington is almost a small town, and the base for the Yorkshire Dales National Park Authority, and is noted for its charming main street and attractive buildings. But perhaps the loveliest part of the dale is where the river flows sedately around the ruined remains of Bolton Priory, built in 1154 by Augustinian Canons.

By far the greater part of Wharfedale, however, is pastoral, and given extensively to sheep farming. The dale pastures rise easily to the surrounding fells, and up to the plateaux above, where the call of moorland birds is borne constantly on the wind. It is, not surprisingly, this mélange of attractive, sheltered dale, gently rising fellsides and high, rolling moorland that makes Wharfedale outstanding walking country.

For those with an interest in industrial archaeology, the landscape of Wharfedale abounds in the remains of the lead mining era, once prolific here. For historians there is a social history in Wharfedale that spans centuries, from the days of Iron Age man and before. There is a vast richness of flora and fauna that will delight natural historians, and a simple beauty that will please anyone.

# 8 Grassington Moors

*This wild walk onto the moors above Grassington is best reserved for a clear day. It makes use of the Dales Way in places and sections of ancient packhorse trails, finally descending to Hebden and the River Wharfe.*

**Distance:** *10 miles/16km*
**Height gain:** *950ft/290m*
**Walking time:** *5 hours*
**Type of walk:** *A sharp contrast between lush*
*valley walking and windswept moorland*
**Start/Finish:** *Grassington village car park GR003637*

Setting off on a section of the Dales Way, head up the main street in Grassington to the town hall. Here, at a crossroads, turn left along Chapel Street, following this to the outskirts of the village. When the lane turns sharply left, leave it for a signposted path entering a farmyard on the right. This leads to a track through a farm gate after the last building. Continue beyond the gate, following a wall, to arrive at three gates in close proximity. Take the middle one, and cross the ensuing field to a narrow gap stile at the far end. Descend a little into the next pasture and curve round, left, to another narrow stile in the far wall. Cross the next enclosed field to yet another stile, giving access to the broad expanse of Lea Green, a vast field system of an ancient British settlement, thought to be Iron Age.

Once on the edge of Lea Green a broad track is crossed as you continue ahead on a green track up a slight rise — ignore any paths going left. Soon a wall appears on the right and, at a distance, escorts the path through low limestone outcrops until the two come together at a stile in the far corner of the field.

Cross the stile and the next field, skirting limestone outcrops on the left, and crossing a ruined wall to a gate on the left. Then cross a series of fields and stiles to level pastures that precede an easy pull to the head of Conistone Dib, a natural, dry gorge descending steeply on the left. Ignore the stile near the top of Conistone Dib, and continue ahead across a bridge to enter a short enclosed section to a gate giving onto the top end of an old packhorse road, Scot Gate Lane, at the point at which it continues north-eastwards as Bycliffe Road.

Turn right on Bycliffe Road, which you now follow for about a mile/1.5km. The road is a well-defined rough-graded track, a wide drove road between walls, and at one point it swings to the right (signposted: Middlesmoor), at a junction with Conistone Turf Road. Keep following the surfaced track through bends and gates, crossing the highest point of the moor, and then descending until level with a dilapidated wall running off at right angles to the right. Turn right along the wall, but gradually bearing away from it on a narrow path, crossing another collapsing wall and continuing on an obvious path. The track runs on to meet a stile over a wall, and continues clearly across the next stretch of moorland to meet two gates. Go through the one on the left, and along a walled green lane.

The lane ends at a gate. Through the gate go half right on a broad grassy track across moorland soon joining another track running beside a wall. Go past a signpost for Conistone, and continue along a vehicle track heading for what looks like a ruined building on the skyline ahead, but which turns out to be a walled lane. Follow this until it eventually turns down to Yarnbury Farm, from where you can make a direct escape straight down the road to Grassington.

Opposite the farm turn left on a bridleway (signposted: Hebden). When the track forks branch right. A short way on you enter an area of mine workings. Keep forward at this point, ignoring all branching tracks to the right. At a gate go left and follow the track as it zigzags down to Hebden Beck. Follow the beck down towards the village.

As you reach the outskirts of Hebden, the track swings across the beck by a bridge. Through a gate, go forward past cottages onto a surfaced lane.

At the crossroads in the village go forward to pass the post office and Methodist church. The lane descends until finally you come in sight of the

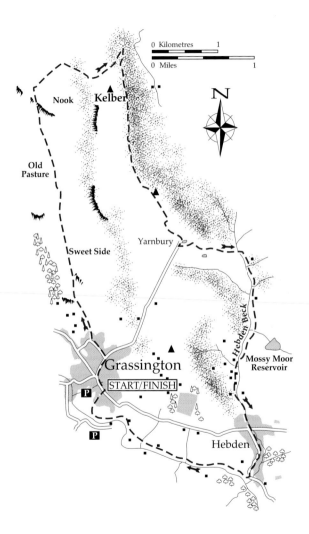

Nook

Kelber

Old
Pasture

Sweet Side

Yarnbury

N

Grassington

START/FINISH

P

P

Hebden Beck

Mossy Moor
Reservoir

Hebden

0 Kilometres 1

0 Miles 1

River Wharfe, and at a low point leave the lane, on the right, through a gate on a signposted track for Grassington Bridge, which takes you down to meet the Dales Way again. Turn right and continue along the north bank of the river, through an avenue of trees — chestnut, beech and oak. When this ends you emerge to see the river set off in a loop. Here head across pastures (and a footbridge) to reach a gate and stile leading onto a broad access road.

Directly ahead, across the Wharfe, stands Linton's church of St Michael and All Angels, a most attractive and unique church, originally reached by a line of stepping stones.

Keep on along the access road until, at a bend, you can cross a stile leading onto a path on the left, heading back to the Wharfe and Linton Falls. The falls, which are quite spectacular after rain, can be viewed from the Tin Bridge, so called from the sound of mill workers' clogs resounding on the sheets of metal that covered one of the earlier bridges here.

Just at the bridge you reach Sedber Lane. Turn right here to walk back up to the car park in Grassington.

# 9 The Monk's Trod

*Although they have succumbed in part to modern alternative uses, all the major routes used on this walk were once important monastic ways, either linking estates or serving granges built on the open fellsides. One is now the Arncliffe to Malham road, while another is usurped by the Pennine Way. The most delightful, however, is still called 'The Monk's Road' on maps.*

| | |
|---|---|
| **Distance:** 8½ miles /13.5km | road walking initially, then excellent moorland tracks |
| **Height gain:** 1,080ft /330m | **Start/Finish:** Arncliffe village. GR931718 (limited parking) |
| **Walking time:** 4-5 hours | |
| **Type of walk:** Lengthy | |

*The Monk's Road, or Trod, was a prominent packhorse route that also served a grange belonging to Fountains Abbey, now the site of derelict Middle House. This splendid traverse sweeps across the moors, high above the limestone escarpment of Yew Cogar before descending steeply into walled lanes that lead back to Arncliffe.*

From Arncliffe walk up Brootes Lane, the road to Malham, in the company of Cowside Beck. Initially the going is steeply uphill, and care needs to be taken against approaching traffic, but as the shoulder of Nab End is reached, so the gradient eases and the views decidedly improve. Beyond Nab End the road descends to Darnbrook House, another abbey grange, and then continues towards Malham. Follow the road until you meet the Pennine Way (though there are no obvious signs of it) at the entrance to Tennant Gill Farm, a National Trust property.

Opposite the farm access, turn left at a wall corner onto a grassy track heading across open pasture. The track descends into an unseen hollow where a wall is crossed by a through stile before rising easily to a wall corner (signpost), and there turns right to run roughly parallel with the wall.

The path passes round Great Hill Farm, and a short way further on, just past a barn, keep forward with a wall on your right. Cross another wall by a stile/gate to enter a grassy valley that leads to the buildings at Water Houses. At a gate you meet a lane serving Malham Tarn House. Turn left and soon enter the Malham Tarn National Nature Reserve consisting of the tarn and its surrounding wetlands, which have international importance, as well as calcareous grassland, woodland and limestone pavement.

The track goes round the back of Malham Tarn House and runs on down a broad, surfaced track, finally leaving the grounds at a cattle grid. As you leave, quit the on-going track and ascend steeply left (signposted) for Middle House. Rise to a higher signpost and then turn right along a clear track that goes on to cross the broad, grassy north-west

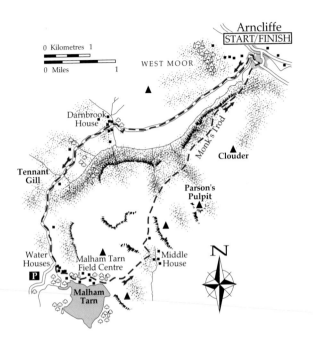

ridge of Great Close Hill: just here you have started on the Monk's Road.

The track runs on, descending towards Middle House Farm. When you cross a step stile over a fence, go half left on a rising grassy path that crosses the shoulder of a small hill, keeping well to the north of Middle House Farm.

The path leads up to a stile over a wall/gate nearby,

beyond which you continue on a broad track for about 200yds/m, when it swings to the right. Follow this towards a small stand of trees enfolding the uninhabited Middle House. Beyond, the track continues to a signpost where it forks. Branch right (signposted for Arncliffe). Some way on, at a wall and stile, you leave the Malham Tarn Estate, as the Monk's Road continues clearly across the sloping upland pastures of Dew Bottoms.

A short way on, when the track forks, keep left, passing a cairn, the first of a few. From here you begin the steady descent to Arncliffe. Eventually, as the path descends, the field patterns on West Moor to the north make an attractive picture, and soon the grey-roofed cottages of the village come into view, huddled around an elongated village green.

The path finally comes down to a gate giving access to a walled lane. Turn left and follow this into the village. It enters the village beside the Falcon pub. Go forward and turn left to return to the foot of Brootes Lane.

# 10 Beamsley Beacon

*Beamsley Beacon, an excellent vantage point, is one of a chain of beacons used throughout England to warn of disasters or invasions. The hill is more properly called Howber Hill, and its ascent is a popular outing, usually from Ilkley or Addingham. Here the ascent is made from Bolton Abbey in order to include a visit to the village of Storiths on the return.*

**Distance:** *6 miles/9.5km*
**Height gain:***1,015ft /310m*
**Walking time:** *4 hours*
**Type of walk:** *Easy*

*walking; some on country lanes*
**Start/Finish:** *Bolton Abbey Estate car park GR071539*

Leave the car park at the exit near the information kiosk and turn right to pass the village green. Cross the road with care, and go forward through the Hole in the Wall, beyond which Bolton Priory comes into view. Go down a broad flight of steps and, as you approach the bottom, bear right across a sloping field to wander down to the riverbank.

Now simply follow the riverbank, which here forms part of the Dales Way. When the path reaches the edge of Bolton Abbey cricket field, continue on an obvious green track to reach the A59 at Bolton Bridge.

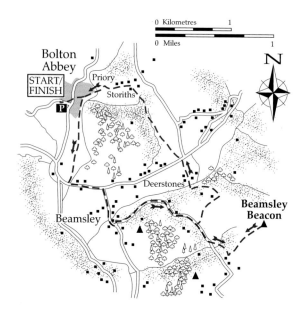

'Old' Bolton Bridge, although still intact, has now been replaced by a 1993 version, but there has been a bridge at this point of the river since 1318. Before then the river would have been crossed by ferry.

Go left across the old bridge, forward to join the new line of the A59, and soon turn right into Beamsley Lane. When you reach Beamsley village, take the road to the left (signposted: Langbar), and follow it up the steep hill that follows. As you come to the top of the road you will see a sign for Beamsley Beacon directing you to follow a wall to meet the main track across the hill. Or you can go further up the road and turn left between two houses on a signposted track leading to the beacon trig pillar.

Having appreciated the extensive view, go back to the lane and down it to take a path on the right leading to Ling Chapel Farm. Keep on past the farm, cross Kex Beck by a footbridge, and walk on to Deerstones, from where an access road leads out to meet the A59 once more.

Cross the road, go left a little, and then set off along the footpath to Storiths. Keep following paths through fields to a stile at the lane below Storiths Crag. Stay on the lane, ahead, through Banks Farm, and then change direction to go down to the top of woodland above the Wharfe.

Follow a descending path to the right, turning left at the bottom to reach the footbridge spanning the Wharfe near Bolton Priory. Across the river follow the broad path back to the Hole in the Wall, and from there return to the car park.

# 11 The Strid

*The Strid woodlands are a superb habitat for wild birds and a wide range of animal and plant life, especially so in spring and early summer, but a remarkable and pleasing place to visit at any time of the year.*

**Distance:** *6 miles/9.5km*
**Height gain:** *Negligible*
**Walking time:** *2-3 hours*
**Type of walk:** *Undemanding, but care is* *needed in the vicinity of The Strid Gorge*
**Start/Finish:** *Bolton Abbey Estate car park. GR071539*

Leave the Bolton Abbey car park at the end furthest from the main entrance, and turn right to pass the village green, heading for the Hole in the Wall. Go down the steps beyond, and the broad track that leads past the ruined remains of Bolton Priory to the footbridge spanning the River Wharfe.

*Just upstream of the bridge can still be seen a line of stepping stones which would have been used to cross the river before the bridge was constructed.*

Over the bridge go left with the on-going path to cross a broad grassy expanse formed by a river loop. Soon you enter delightful woodland at a stile. Keep ahead at all times and you will eventually come out onto a minor road, Hazelwood Lane, near Pickles Beck.

Cross the beck and turn immediately left on a path heading back towards the river. Turn right on a signposted path through a gap stile, and onto a broad path leading to the bridge at Cavendish Pavilion. Cross the bridge and turn right, going forward into Strid Wood.

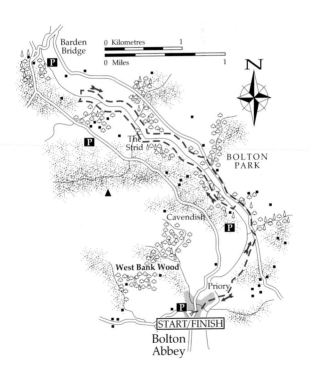

Having entered the wood keep going ahead, ignoring deviations left and right, until you arrive at an information board close by The Strid Gorge. You will need to divert to have a close look at the gorge, but be warned, the rocks are slippery and the gorge a treacherous place in which people have been killed in recent times. Keep a safe distance away.

Continue with the on-going path which climbs a little before returning to the river. At a junction, follow the path ahead, cross an arched bridge, and finally leave the woodland at a stile and gate.

Walk across grassy riverside embankments to reach an old aqueduct spanning the river by means of which you can cross to the opposite (true left) bank once more, in so doing taking your leave of the Dales Way.

Turn right once across the river and pursue an obvious path back into woodland that echoes in spring to birdsong. Continue to follow the course of the river, but, for much of the way, rather higher above it than on the opposite bank. The woodland here, however, is much richer, and more likely to reward you with sight of some of its wide range of birds and animals.

*Strid Wood is renowned for its wealth of flora and fauna. Most of the trees are broad-leaved, with some specimens as much as 300 years old. They support over sixty species of nesting bird and, unusually, over eighty species of lichen — more than double what you might expect to find elsewhere. Other important surveys list ninety-seven species of fungi, forty of mollusca, forty-one liverworts, and ninety-eight mosses — an amazing array by any standards.*

Shortly after the path returns to riverside level, it rises to meet a country lane which takes you on to cross Posforth Beck. A short way further on you return to the wooded confines of the river. A good, clear path leads you finally out of the woodland and into an open meadow as once more you approach Cavendish Bridge.

From the bridge (without crossing it, unless you want refreshments), continue ahead to retrace your outward steps to Bolton Priory and up to the Hole in the Wall, and the car park.

# 12 Barden Fell

*In spite of an off-putting name, this walk through the Valley of Desolation is one walk that every visitor to Wharfedale should do. On it you will ascend through a deer park, where the last of the indigenous red deer of Wharfedale were held captive, and climb beside attractive waterfalls to the high heathered moors of Barden Fell*

**Distance:** 8 miles/13km
**Height gain:** 1,245ft /380m
**Walking time:** 4-5 hours
**Type of walk:** A

*moderately demanding walk onto a high moor. No dogs permitted*
**Start/Finish:** *Cavendish Pavilion car park* GR077552

Leave the Cavendish Pavilion and cross the river, turning right into a field to follow a riverside path which soon enters and then leaves some trees near Posforth Bridge. Turn sharp right, and walk up the road for a short distance to Waterfall Cottage, and here leave the road by a gate leading to a clear track uphill to the edge of Access Land. Aim half left across a field, passing a couple of venerable oak trees to a gate in a corner.

From the gate a path goes across to Posforth Gill. The main path keeps above the gill, but a short detour down to it will reveal a splendid cascade. Return to the main path and continue to follow it

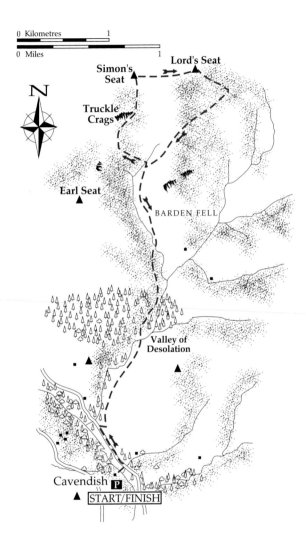

0 Kilometres 1

0 Miles 1

**N**

Lord's Seat ▲

Simon's Seat ▲

Truckle Crags

Earl Seat ▲

BARDEN FELL

Valley of Desolation

▲

▲

Cavendish **P**

▲ START/FINISH

69

through the Valley of Desolation to a footbridge where you can cross the stream.

*The Valley of Desolation is so named because of the devastation caused by a major landslip during a storm in the early 1800s. Fortunately, the worst of the damage has now been concealed.*

Now keep going along the north side of the gill to a fork, and here branch left to a stile into Laund Pasture Plantation. There is, however, another attractive waterfall awaiting anyone who branches right for a short distance, when the path forks.

Through the plantation a good path leads to a gate giving onto the open moors.

*The moors are part of the Barden Fell and Barden Moor Access Area where you can generally wander at will. This means, however, that although the moors are open for most of the year, they can be (and are) closed during times when grouse shooting takes place (between August and December), or at times of high fire risk. In fact, once you leave the road at Posforth Bridge all the paths are permissive, and not rights of way. This need to protect the moorland and the grouse that inhabit it also means that dogs are not allowed into the access area.*

As you leave the plantation the path continues directly ahead, and leads clearly all the way to the top of Simon's Seat. En route you cross Great Agill Beck at a ford, and go past a stone table that is an ideal spot for a picnic break. From here you can see the top of Simon's Seat for the first time.

Higher up, the path crosses the feeder streams of Great Agill Beck and then swings round below Truckle Crags, from where it is only a few more minutes to the trig pillar on the summit.

*The view from the top of Simon's Seat is quite splendid, extending into Skyreholme, a tributary dale of the Wharfe, to Appletreewick, and up the main valley to Burnsall, as well as further afield.*

The speediest return is to retrace your steps, but there is an alternative. Take a path heading roughly east from the summit to the outcrop known as Lord's Seat. There turn right alongside a wall, and after about 700yds/m of easy descent, turn right onto a broad track. This crosses the moor and leads back to join the outward route not far from the stone table. Now there is no choice but to retrace your steps to Cavendish.

# 13 Capplestone Gate

*This walk provides a wonderful opportunity to inspect the limestone countryside along the eastern flank of Wharfedale. The walk is not difficult, but is best kept for a fine, clear day for reasons that will be apparent when you reach the highest point.*

**Distance:** *7 miles/11km*
**Height gain:** *1,080ft /330m*
**Walking time:** *3-4 hours*
**Type of walk:** *A*

*moderate hill walk, rising almost continually*
**Start/Finish:** *Conistone (very limited parking) GR981675*

*Lovely and charming is the little village of Conistone, thankfully by-passed by the main valley road. It sits across the valley from neighbouring Kilnsey, separated by flats of lush green meadow that were once a large post-glacial lake. Behind Kilnsey is its famous crag, while behind Conistone rise two conspicuous knolls, Wassa Hill and Conistone Pie.*

*The villages are both of early foundation. Conistone is recorded in the Domesday Book as land held by Gospatric. Many of the datestones and decorated doorheads found in the village, however, date from the 17th century. Being built from local stone, they meld harmoniously with the surrounding landscape. The church of St Mary in Conistone was largely rebuilt in*

*Victorian times, but retains parts that are Norman.*

*As you will see, on the limestone plateau above Conistone there are many signs — hut circles, farmsteads and field systems — of prehistoric settlements, largely dating from the Iron Age.*

Parking in Conistone is very limited. It may be possible to park near Wharfe Bridge, or you can begin the walk from Kilnsey.

Start down the road towards Kettlewell, but immediately leave it to turn right onto a track through a wide village green. Adjoining the last house you will find three gates; take the middle one and bear right. On an improving path, climb into the dry valley of Conistone Dib, ascending through its narrow confines to emerge at a stile into a long, narrow field. Cross the field to another stile.

When the Dib closes in higher up, keep following a wall until a brief rocky interlude spurs you on to the top. Cross a wall by a stile, beyond which a short scramble places you in the open at last. Cross another stile, and turn left along a track to a gate. Through this gate you reach an old packhorse route at the junction of Scot Gate Lane and Bycliffe Road. Turn right.

Soon after passing through a gate, Bycliffe Road bends sharply right. Leave the track at this point, going through a gate on the left and onto Conistone Turf Road. Soon, the way bends right

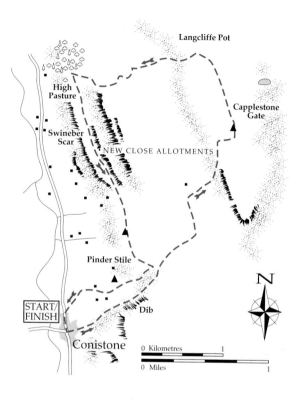

Langcliffe Pot

High
Pasture

Swineber
Scar

NEW CLOSE ALLOTMENTS

Capplestone
Gate

Pinder Stile

START/
FINISH

Dib

Conistone

N

0 Kilometres          1

0 Miles               1

again through a gate, near a plantation. Keep to
the right of the plantation, and then head across
the next field, aiming for the northerly end of a
prominent scar. Beyond this the gradient eases
significantly as the trig pillar on Capplestone Gate
comes into view.

*In this top section of the walk you exchange the brightness of limestone for the dour greys of gritstone that have survived erosion, and this comes as something of a surprise. What may also be a surprise is the extent of the panorama from the top of Capplestone Gate; it is an outstanding viewpoint and embraces Yockenthwaite Moor, Fountains Fell, Pen-y-ghent and Pendle Hill.*

From the trig pillar cross the stile by a nearby gate and turn left along a path close by a wall to go through an area of lead mine workings. Further on, just after a cairn, you can cross the wall at a stile. The ensuing descent is initially steep, but soon eases as it passes through a collapsed wall. Continue downwards, the path forking indistinctly at one point (either way will do), and rejoining not far above a gate in a lower wall.

Immediately through the gate follow a descending path to meet a level path lower down near a plantation boundary. This is the Dales Way. If you now turn sharp left, you can follow it through a succession of pastures and stiles to visit Coniston Pie (an excellent place to put your feet up and enjoy the scenery).

A short way further on you reach the junction between Scot Gate Lane and Bycliffe Road. Here, rather than descend through Coniston Dib, turn right, before the wall, and go down Scot Gate Lane. At a wall junction go through a gate and continue down the lane, which later becomes surfaced as it goes down Wassa Bank. When you reach the road at the bottom, turn left to return to the village centre.

# 14 Linton Falls

*This short, charming and easy walk visits the unique Linton Church, the village of Linton itself, and the neighbouring community of Threshfield before concluding at Linton Falls, the largest waterfall on the River Wharfe. Along the way you will encounter some splendid examples of early cultivation terraces, thought to date from the 13th century.*

| | |
|---|---|
| **Distance:** *3½ miles /5.5km* | **Type of walk:** *Easy paths and tracks* |
| **Height gain:** *195ft/60m* | **Start/Finish:** *Linton Falls car park GR002632* |
| **Walking time:** *2-2½ hours* | |

Leave the car park and enter the church grounds. Whether you intend to visit the church now or at the end of the walk, you should allow ample time to look around it.

*St Michael and All Angels' Church must be one of the most individual of Dales' churches. Like Bolton Priory, it occupies a bend in the river, though Linton Church is much nearer the water, its churchyard valiantly clinging to the riverbank. It dates from the 12th century, possibly during the period of church building that characterised Henry II's reign (1154-1189), and is very squat without a tower. The church was extensively altered in the 14th century, but it still retains parts of the earlier church.*

Exit the churchyard at the far corner by a path leading to the stepping stones across the Wharfe by means of which parishioners used to make their way to church. Turn right, along the riverbank to cross a stile, and climb behind a small woodland, then cross two fields to reach the B6160.

Cross the road and follow a signposted way up the ensuing field to a wooden gate.

*On the way you get a good view of some ancient cultivation terraces — lynchets — in the adjoining fields. These were constructed to improve the condition of the land.*

When you reach Thorpe Lane, a quiet country lane, turn right for about 100yds/m to a step stile on the right. Over this you follow a signposted route down through the lynchets to a ladder stile, beyond which a track runs down to Linton village.

Linton Beck flows through the village green, which can be crossed by one of three different bridges — a clapper bridge, a packhorse bridge and a modern road bridge. Leave the village along the left bank of Linton Beck, heading for Threshfield. The footpath leads down to an old lane that rounds Linton House and crosses fields to reach a humped bridge over a disused railway line — part of the Yorkshire Dales Railway from Skipton to Grassington, which was completed in 1902.

Keep ahead from the bridge, alongside a wall. Then, at the next field, head diagonally across to reach Threshfield, there turning right over Threshfield Bridge.

*The village of Threshfield used to have a reputation for making 'besoms', i.e. brooms made from twigs of heather.*

Go along the road opposite the Old Hall Inn to reach the B6160 again. Turn right for a short distance, and take the second path on the left, signposted to Threshfield School. The path follows the line of a lynchet to another footbridge, also spanning the disused railway. Turn left for 200yds/m and then take the riverside path on the right to Linton Falls.

Cross an in-flowing mill stream by Little Emily's Bridge, when a left turn brings you to the Wharfe and soon its splendid falls.

*Little Emily's Bridge is a small packhorse bridge on the original church path from Threshfield. It dates from the 14th century, and is thought to have been named after a member of the Norton family, who took refuge nearby at the time of the Civil War. There is another suggestion that it is purely the invention of novelist Halliwell Sutcliffe whose works during the early years of the 20th century drew from the rich seam of life that inhabited this region, and introduced many people to places they had never known or knew existed.*

Go onto the bridge across the Wharfe for an excellent view of Linton Falls, and then go back and continue the short distance down the road to the car park.

*Linton Falls are a fine spectacle and occur along the Craven Fault line. The present bridge is the fourth to occupy this position. The first, known as the Tin Bridge, was built in 1814 by the Birkbecks for workers at Linton Mill. It was covered with sheets of metal from old oil drums, and this is what gave it its name. A second bridge replaced the original in 1860, and a third in 1904. This became dangerous and was closed in 1988, being replaced by the present bridge a year later.*

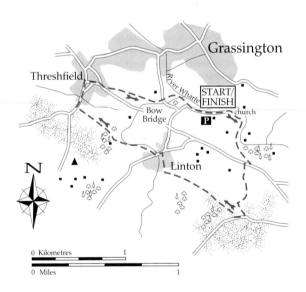

# 15 Trollers Gill

*This easy walk takes in delectable river scenery and explores the fascinating limestone landscape of Wharfedale. It also visits the lair of a legendary hound of death.*

| | |
|---|---|
| **Distance:** *6 miles/9.5km* | *moderate walk through* |
| **Height gain:** *525ft/160m* | *limestone country* |
| **Walking time:** *4 hours* | **Start/Finish:** |
| **Type of walk**: *A* | *Appletreewick. GR053601* |

The walk begins in Appletreewick (formerly, but no longer so I'm told, pronounced Ap'trick locally) by taking a path from near the centre of the village that runs down to the River Wharfe, through a field that in summer is used for parking. At the river turn left.

*Appletreewick is a modest-sized place, but has a number of claims to fame. It is a one street village, a street lined with fine old buildings on both sides. High Hall has a minstrel gallery in its main room, while Mock Beggar Hall, originally known as Monk's Hall, housed the monks in charge of Bolton Priory's property in the area.*

*Among Appletreewick's citizens William Craven especially rose to considerable importance. In 1562 he was sent to London to be an apprentice to a merchant*

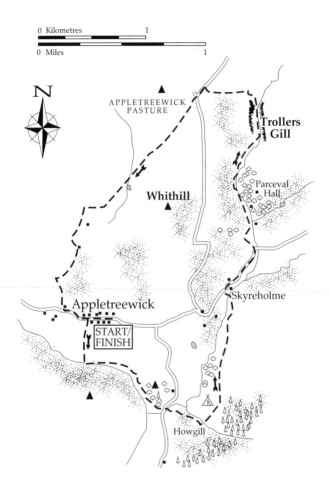

0 Kilometres 1

0 Miles 1

N

APPLETREEWICK
PASTURE

Trollers
Gill

Whithill

Parceval
Hall

Appletreewick

Skyreholme

START/
FINISH

Howgill

*tailor. By the time he was 21 he had become a member of the Merchant Taylor's Guild, and in due course entered into business at a mansion house in Watling Street. He became increasingly successful and popular, and in 1594 donated £50 (then an enormous sum) towards the building of St John's College, Oxford. In 1600 he was elected Alderman for Bishopgate, and a year later was chosen Sheriff of London. He was knighted by James I in 1603, and in 1611 became Lord Mayor of London — a real life Dick Whittington, in fact!*

A short diversion over a stile on the left leads to a wooden staircase from the top of which you descend back to the company of the river. Continue through another meadow and a pleasant stretch of woodland at the end of which, through a gate, you head left across a field to join a track out to a lane, meeting it beside a bridge.

Cross the bridge and take a walled track rising on the left. Shortly, at a crossroads at Howgill turn left up Howgill Lane and go past a caravan site at Howgill Lodge.

*Howgill itself is a scattered community at the foot of Simon's Seat. In the 14th century it was the site of one of the six hunting lodges that comprised the ancient Chase of Barden.*

A short way further on, opposite an old milestone, turn left through a gateway, following a wall, and then switching sides of it. At another gate, aim for a stile beyond, then descend to cross a tiny stream following which there is a further stile. Stay along the line of the main stream, Fir Beck, on your left to a collapsed wall and footbridge. Cross the footbridge and climb to meet a lane, at Skyreholme.

Turn right, up the lane, and continue until it forks near a bridge. Here turn left to reach the entrance to Parceval Hall.

*The Hall was built in the 17th century, but has an Elizabethan look about it. It is commonly regarded as the finest residential building in Wharfedale (now used as a retreat), and its gardens are open to the public during the summer months.*

Just before a wooden bridge go through a gate and follow Skyreholme Beck upstream, passing a large grass-covered mound that once formed the dam of a large reservoir serving the Skyreholme paper mills.

Eventually you reach a wall in front of the entrance to Trollers Gill, with the lump of Middle Hill on the left. Go right, to enter the gill.

*Trollers Gill is a miniature gorge through the Great Scar limestone. Although more than 300yds/m long, the gill is narrow, dark and steep-sided. In its depths you will find the lair of the Barguest, the spectral hound of Craven, a huge shaggy beast, yellow, with eyes as big as saucers. Legend has it that an encounter with the Barguest usually meant death — so be warned!*

At the far end, where a wall descends to the gill, climb up to the left and over a stile across a fence. Beyond, drop to meet a path just above Gill Head Mine. Unless you wish to visit the mine, now disused, turn right along its old access track, and when it swings sharply right, leave it, and keep straight ahead. Pass a small pot hole (Hell Hole), cross a stretch of ground that is often wet, and head for a wall, beyond which you reach a road.

Go left to a gate on the right (signposted: Hartlington), beyond which a wide stony track leads out across the moor, level at first and then slowly descending, crossing two stiles on the way. The track eventually becomes a green lane, and when, near a field corner, you meet a crosspath, take the left path for Appletreewick. This is a winding track from which there are excellent views of the numerous reef knolls that form the landscape along the North Craven Fault.

# 16 Birks Fell Ridge

*South-west from Buckden rises the tumescent mound of Birks Fell, separating Wharfedale and Langstrothdale from Littondale, without which this walk would be a comparatively simple affair. As it is, while the generous helping of ascent and descent injects its own brand of interest, there is no escaping the fact that here is a walk of great beauty, offering views of many old Dales' favourites from a different perspective.*

| | |
|---|---|
| **Distance:** *11¼ miles /18km* | *winter. The ridge crossing has to be repeated later in the day* |
| **Height gain:** *2,430ft /740m* | **Start/Finish:** *Buckden car park* |
| **Walking time:** *6-7 hours* | |
| **Type of walk:** *Demanding, especially in* | *GR942774 (car park charge)* |

*The Wharfedale village of Buckden marks the point where the valley changes direction and assumes another identity, becoming thereafter known as Langstrothdale. The Dales Way marches through here, a fairly reliable indicator of the high quality of the walking to be enjoyed in the dale.*

Begin from the car park in Buckden and head for the village, but turn immediately right on the road to Hubberholme. Just after Buckden Bridge, take to the signposted Dales Way on a riparian loop before rejoining the road not far from Hubberholme.

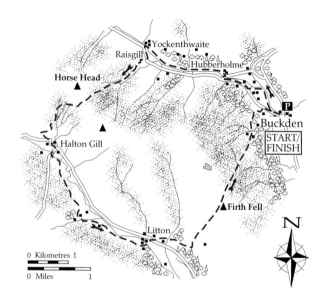

Two hundred years ago, the Wharfe bridge was known as Election Bridge, following a speech by a prospective Member of Parliament in which a new bridge was promised in return for votes. The votes were cast and the bridge came about, but only at the expense of much-needed repairs to Hubberholme Bridge. Although Hubberholme Bridge was subsequently repaired, the Skipton Quarter Sessions in 1639 learned that it was in "great ruyne and decay", a significant cause for concern since it lay on "the high roade way leading between the markett towne of Lancaster and the markett towne of Newcastle upon Tyne".

The church of St Michael and All Angels in

*Hubberholme is a real attraction. Originally, the church here was built as a forest chapel, but in 1241 was given to the monks of Coverham Abbey. During the 19th century the church at Hubberholme was a chapel-of-ease to the mother church, then at Arncliffe. The present building contains one of only two remaining rood lofts in Yorkshire, as well as two altars, one of which was coveted by a former landlord-cum-parish clerk who had it removed to the nearby George Inn as an ale bench.*

At Hubberholme, cross the bridge and go behind the church to continue northwards on the true left bank of the river as far as Yockenthwaite, where another bridge lets you return along the road the short distance to the neat assemblage of cottages and farms at Raisgill. From here an ancient monastic way and packhorse route leaves the road and swings up onto Horse Head Moor, roughly following the line of Hagg Beck, with improving views as you ascend.

A long, but steady ascent follows as you climb to Horse Head Gate, where a splendid panorama awaits — Darnbrook Fell, Fountains Fell, Pen-y-ghent and Plover Hill all superimpose themselves on the more distant but familiar profiles of Ingleborough and Whernside.

*Horse Head Gate is the point of no return, and from it a long descent leads to Halton Gill, so a decision on whether you have the strength or disposition needed to carry you down to the valley, along the Skirfare to Litton and then back up and over to Buckden, is important before leaving this high threshold. If in doubt, simply retrace your steps. Incidentally, although the ridge you are crossing has for many years been called Birks Fell Ridge — because Birks Fell was long considered to be the highest point — in fact the summit Horse Head, just a short distance away, is higher.*

Otherwise, it is helter-skelter downhill, with the first glimpses of field-patterned Littondale expanding as you descend into an attractive landscape: this is Kingsley's 'Vendale' of *The Water Babies*, and was once also known as Amerdale.

*Most of the buildings in Halton Gill date from the 17th century, but in earlier times the village was the hub of many radiating monastic and packhorse trails that once served important peripheral settlements like Hawes, Bainbridge, Middleham, Horton-in-Ribblesdale and Settle. Indeed, the monastic route from Ribblesdale to Halton Gill is one of the best known in the Dales, serving the lands owned by Sawley Abbey above Langcliffe and Stainforth.*

For a short distance follow the road towards Stainforth until you can cross Halton Gill Bridge, beyond which a good path leads across fields to Nether Heselden and Pen-y-ghent Gill, to cross the River Skirfare by a footbridge at Litton. Here the village, by no means the largest settlement, has loaned its name to the whole valley.

*The Queen's Arms pub on a hot summer's day is altogether too tempting, especially with the long haul back to Buckden awaiting: in winter its hospitality is just irresistible.*

Beside the pub a signposted bridleway leads to a green rake slanting upwards across the fellside, first crossing Crystal Beck and then continuing to tackle the steep hillside obliquely. Finally, it changes direction and heads arrow-straight for the top of the ridge, which is reached near the trig pillar on Firth Fell.

From the ridge the final downhill is engaged. Begin for a short distance by following the line of a wall, then pass through a gap in it to head for woodlands that surround Redmires Farm, a long and steady descent with Buckden, embraced protectively in the folds of Buckden Beck, seeming to come no nearer. Eventually, however, a farm track drops quickly to Redmires and back onto the minor road to Hubberholme just west of Buckden Bridge, from where a simple stroll leads back into Buckden.

# 17 Starbotton

*Only from a position above the valley can you fully appreciate how Wharfedale has been fashioned by the Ice Age, and how well, today, Kettlewell fits into its place. This energetic walk allows you to gain height and to appreciate the landscape, concluding with an easy stroll alongside the River Wharfe from the smaller, upstream village of Starbotton.*

**Distance:** *6¼ miles/10km*
**Height gain:** *1,065ft /325m*
**Walking time:** *4 hours*
**Type of walk:** *Steep and energetic start, followed by easy walking: on good paths throughout*
**Start/Finish:** *Kettlewell bridge car park. GR969723*

*The delightful, jumbled village of Kettlewell which occupies the east bank of the River Wharfe cannot be much different today from how it was three or four hundred years ago. There is some uncertainty about the origin of its name, some authorities linking it with an Irish-Norse chieftain, Ketel. The village is certainly old, and pre-dates the Domesday Survey in 1086, though the Domesday recorders noted little that might tell us what the community was like in the 11th century.*

Leave the car park and walk left into the village. Cross the bridge in front of the Bluebell Hotel and turn right, following the road to a junction near the post office.

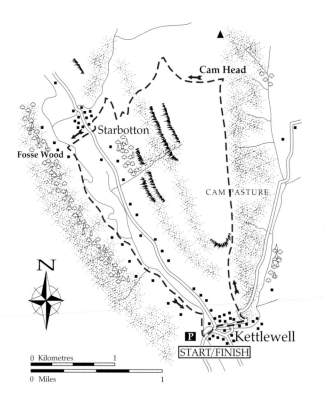

Keep ahead at the junction, onto the minor road to Leyburn, an old packhorse trail, and shortly turn left to climb a steep gradient. Within a few minutes, when the Leyburn road bends to the right, leave it for the easier gradient of a broad track between walls, signposted to Cam Head. This is Top Mere Road, and its ascent is initially still quite demanding before it finally relents, rising arrow-straight up the tongue of ground between the Wharfe and Cam Gill.

When eventually you break free of the enclosing walls there comes an invigorating sense of openness as the track presses on to meet another old track, Starbotton Cam Road, just before a small hummock. It was here, on the slopes of Tor Mere Top, that the people living in the valley came to dig peat for their fires, hauling the dried peats by cart and pony back down to the valley.

Go left here and follow the track as it descends westwards, with splendid views over the dale below and to the rising hillsides beyond, to the village of Starbotton.

*Starbotton is a compact assortment of 17th- and 18th-century houses, many a legacy of the lead mining era. Today it is best remembered for the devastation it sustained on the 8th June 1686, when a terrible storm turned Cam Gill Beck behind the village into a raging torrent, sending boulders and slurry down the hillside, sweeping away or damaging many of the houses. This was the worst flooding ever experienced in the valley.*

As you come down to Starbotton go left through the streets and onto the main valley road, the B6160. At the southern end of the village you can cross the road to follow a path going down to the Wharfe, which is crossed by a footbridge.

Once over the Wharfe, turn left, and follow the

river towards Kettlewell. The way back alongside the river is obvious, you are on the Dales Way, finally leaving the river briefly to climb to Kettlewell bridge, with the car park just beyond.

# 18 Buckden Pike

*Buckden Pike is the second highest summit in Wharfedale and, for those who like to bag such summits, a 'Marilyn'. Its ascent is a popular and uncomplicated walk, and although on the ground a footpath runs southwards from the summit to allow a link with Kettlewell, there is no right of way. For this reason, this has to be an out-and-back walk, but it is no less enjoyable for that.*

| | |
|---|---|
| **Distance:** 4³/₄ miles / 7.5km | **Type of walk:** *A moderately demanding uphill walk* |
| **Height gain:** 1,510ft/ 460m | **Start/Finish:** *Buckden village car park. GR942774* |
| **Walking time:** 3¹/₂ hours | |

*The settlement of Buckden is a Norman foundation, set up as part of the medieval hunting forest of Langstrothe, and originally the creation of the Percys of Northumberland. Years ago, the village was a bustling place, the last village in Wharfedale. In those former times, when population movement took people from the Dales to places like the Lancashire coast, returning Dalesfolk coming home from holidays could take a coach as far as Buckden from where they walked across the hillsides to Wensleydale and Swaledale.*

*The village used to boast three inns: the 'Low Cock', in a yard opposite Buckden House, was the first to go, while the white house up a lane at the top end of the village was formerly the 'High Cock'. Now only the 'Buck Inn' remains, and it was here that the farmers used to come to sell their wool.*

The car park is at the northern end of Buckden village, and you leave it by a gate at its top end. This gets you onto a sloping track known as Buckden Rake, which climbs through the sparse trees of Rakes Wood. This is the route of a Roman road over to Wensleydale that ran from Ilkley to Bainbridge.

As you rise beyond the trees you get a good view of Hubberholme and the upper dale,

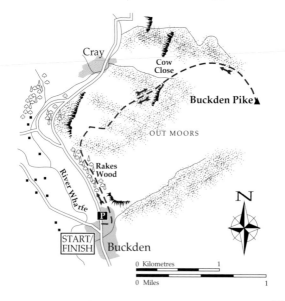

Langstrothdale. At a gate the track levels for a while until you reach a second gate. Here fork right, resuming the upward climb through a succession of gates and pastures.

From the top of the last field the path heads up the open hillside, but you are effectively contained by a wall, and directed straight to the summit.

*The top of Buckden Pike is a fine place to enjoy a picnic break. If it is crowded, cross the stile and walk directly away from the summit for a short distance to gaze down upon the infrequently visited dale of Walden.*

To return, simply retrace your steps.

# 19 Cray and Scar House

*The tiny hamlet of Cray is perched on the steeply descending highway from Aysgarth in Wensleydale. This walk climbs to Cray from Buckden, and then skips across the southern slopes of Yockenthwaite Moor to Scar House, where the Quaker tradition flourished strongly in the 17th and 18th centuries.*

**Distance:** *5 miles/8km*
**Height gain:** *345ft/105m*
**Walking time:** *3-4 hours*
**Type of walk:** *A moderately easy walk on*

*good paths throughout, with splendid views of upper Wharfedale*
**Start/Finish**: *Buckden car park. GR942774*

*Buckden is the 'valley of the bucks', the home of deer since records began. It is an exquisite place, hemmed in by beauty on all sides, a place guaranteed to make a sensitive soul rejoice. Here, for me, is all that is beautiful about the Dales. This walk will give you a glimpse of that beauty, which can be appreciated as much in the depths of winter as it can during the brightness of summer months.*

Leave the car park at the northern end, and start up the broad track that rises easily through Rakes Wood. As a gate is approached the angle of ascent eases, and soon a track deviates uphill towards higher ground. Ignore this, it leads up to Buckden Pike. Instead continue ahead along the level edge of a limestone escarpment.

Soon you reach a wall and gate with a narrow stile to the right. Squeeze through the stile and keep ahead for a short distance to a narrow gate, where

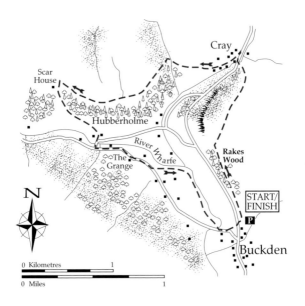

a footpath sign indicates a descent to Cray way below.

*With the benefit of height the whole of the limestone landscape of Upper Wharfedale and Langstrothdale is clearly seen, from the high moorland plateaux to the deep trough in which the juvenile Wharfe ambles sedately along.*

From the gate the descent to Cray is initially steep and leads down beside a wall to a footpath sign, and a short descent to a gate. Just here Cray Gill is encountered, and crossed by a shallow ford, to reach the road. If you need refreshment, the nearby pub will oblige.

Continue behind the pub on a broad farm track (signposted: Stubbing Bridge and Yockenthwaite). Two tracks are encountered, with the higher proving to be the better route, leading to a gate where the onward route to Scar House is signposted.

From the gate the continuation is evident enough, and keeps to the edge of the escarpment, with only one slight deviation to cross Crook Gill by a bridge. Keep ahead along a level grassy ledge.

The on-going path closes in on a wall, and squeezes round its edge directly above Hubberholme, before continuing less evenly and tending right to keep above the intake wall, soon to reach Scar House, once a lively place of worship.

*It was at Scar House that there grew and flourished the new religion of the Quakers, the Society of Friends, largely inspired by George Fox, whose vision on Pendle Hill of "a great people in white raiment by a river side, coming to the Lord" sent him dashing about the northern parts of England preaching the perfectibility of all men through inward personal experience. George Fox is known to have visited Scar House twice, in 1652 and 1677, though whether the remains of Scar House that you see today are similar to those he knew is uncertain.*

From Scar House you descend directly to Hubberholme, there passing round the church and over the Wharfe Bridge to turn left along the road, heading back towards Buckden. Before long you leave the road for a path on the left which loops alongside the Wharfe, a safer option than walking down the road, which is very busy in summer.

Eventually the path does rejoin the road not far from Buckden Bridge, beyond which the village is only a short uphill stroll away.

# 20 Langstrothdale

*This delightful walk from Buckden to Beckermonds entirely follows the Dales Way. The walking is pleasant every step of the way, and, being a linear walk, you have the opportunity of walking every step back again; otherwise you'll need to make transport arrangements.*

**Distance:** 6½ miles /10.5km (one way)
**Height gain:** 280ft/85m
**Walking time:** 3 hours
**Type of walk:** Easy

*riverside rambling*
**Start:** Buckden car park GR942772
**Finish:** Beckermonds GR874803

Not until it reaches Buckden does the River Wharfe significantly begin to turn southwards, bound for Kettlewell, Grassington, Burnsall, Appletreewick, and the larger town of Ilkley.

*The reaches of the Wharfe above Buckden flow through a valley known as Langstrothdale, a name that holds the tang of wild places, where the sound of stags in rut would have echoed across the hoary hillsides on chill October mornings, and at other times the hunted deer would have sidled through the stands of trees like silent shadows. Indeed, Buckden was the home of deer since records began, 'the valley of the bucks', and deer still roamed the slopes of Birks Fell until the early 1950s.*

*Upstream of Buckden, the Wharfe fashions a course from its birthplace high on Cam Fell. Upstream, too, lie the villages and hamlets of Hubberholme, Yockenthwaite, Deepdale and Beckermonds, and this linear walk pays them all a visit. Without transport at both ends the walk means retracing your outward steps, no less a perfectly agreeable experience for doing it the other way round. Or you can simply retreat at any time.*

Leave the national park car park at the northern end of Buckden village, going left, and descend, right, to the Wharfe Bridge, known 200 years ago as Election Bridge, from a speech by a prospective Member of Parliament in which a new bridge was promised in return for votes. The bridge came about, but only at the expense of much-needed repairs to Hubberholme Bridge.

Just after the bridge, take to a broad path on the right that keeps close to the river until it rejoins the road a short distance from Hubberholme. Then simply walk up to the village.

*Hubberholme, part of the manor of Kettlewell at the time of the Domesday survey, has two notable buildings worthy of a visit. One, the George Inn, is the venue for an annual land-letting ceremony held on the first Monday in the New Year, which takes the form of an auction by candlelight, at which bids are made for the use of a pasture owned by the church. The last bid before the candle flickers out becomes the rent payable.*

*The other building, which you reach by crossing Hubberholme Bridge, is its church, St Michael and All Angels, a real attraction. Originally, the church was*

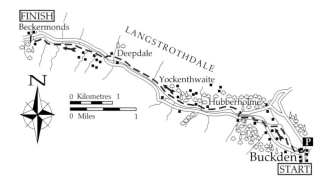

*built as a forest chapel, and in 1241 given to the monks of Coverham Abbey.*

To continue, go through a gate near the church until, beyond the churchyard wall, you can abandon the track leading up to Scar House, to follow a lower path (signposted) across meadowland to regain the Wharfe.

The riverside path is never in doubt, scarcely leaving the river by more than a few metres. Amiably, and with shallow cascades to enliven its progress, it accompanies you to Yockenthwaite, where the path passes through a wall gap, just before the first gate, into sheep enclosures. By more gates you escape sometimes dire underfoot conditions to gain a broad farm track, from which you move diagonally right and slightly uphill towards the main farm buildings, before heading for Deepdale.

*Yockenthwaite is a curious name, found in many guises in the parish registers, wherein one parson describes it simply as Yoke and White, while at other times it has appeared as Yoghannesthweit. This, at least, gives a clue to its meaning, for 'thweit' is a corruption of 'thwaite', meaning a clearing, while 'Yoghannes' comes from an old Irish personal name, Eogan. So, the hamlet name simply means Eogan's Clearing.*

Yockenthwaite Bridge, and the crystal waters beneath, is well worth a moment of your time. To do so simply stay on the main track, but do not cross the bridge. Return instead to the main building, to a signposted path going left to a gate, still continuing along the northern bank of the river.

A short way on, the path passes close by a prehistoric stone circle, once described as a Giant's Grave, though it is now known to have been some kind of Bronze Age burial place.

After the stone circle the track is less pronounced, heading for a stile into an enclosed pasture where an indistinct path rises away from the river, through another wall gap and on to a ladder stile to pass round the edge of a field before reaching a small footbridge spanning Deepdale Gill. A short way on, the access road to Deepdale Farm is reached, and you should follow this out to the valley road, and there cross the Wharfe by Deepdale Bridge.

Beyond Deepdale Bridge a wide path between wall

and river leads on past a footbridge near New House through the most pleasant scenery towards the larger community of Beckermonds.

*Beckermonds, sometimes known as Beggarmans, lies in a sheltered hollow on the edge of Greenfield Forest. It is a truly remote hamlet that predates the Domesday recorders.*

Just south of Beckermonds, the path guides you to a footbridge spanning Greenfield Beck, beyond which a short, walled track takes you up to the access road into Beckermonds, where your transport will be waiting, or from where you must retrace your steps.

# AIREDALE AND MALHAMDALE

The village of Malham used to be a place of considerable importance for the buying and selling of sheep and cattle, most notably during the days when Fountains Abbey and Bolton Priory had granges there. By all accounts it was not unusual to find more than 5,000 cattle pastured there, while the annual Sheep Fair brought more than 100,000 animals into the dale.

Today tourists have replaced sheep and cattle as the main source of the village's economic wealth. They come in their droves to gaze at the soaring cliff walls of the Cove and Gordale Scar, to walk on the limestone pavement above, and to explore the green and white landscape that ripples away in all directions.

It seems to have been ever thus. Thirty years ago Harry Scott, former editor-proprietor of *The Dalesman* magazine, described the scene at Malham on a hot Sunday afternoon, with "fancy-dressed visitors, picnic parties, impromptu dances to the ever-present transistor, family games of cricket, sun-bathers, some earnest elderly walkers who disdain hiking regalia and many pseudo-potholers who carry enough equipment to descend a hundred potholes but who rarely move from the green". Moreover, the village had "a fringe of bicycles, scooters, up-to-the-minute motor cycles and ancient cars".

Well, some things have changed, but not all. Impromptu dances I'm not sure about, nor the family games of cricket. Most visitors to the dale these days come to use it as a base to explore the countryside, and, for the most part, bicycles and scooters have been replaced by cars, cars and more cars — a situation not in the least helped by the grossly inadequate bus service into the dale. Maybe there's a case here for a 'Malham Wanderer', a park-and-ride scheme that would keep all the cars out of the dale, and bus visitors in on a constant shuttle service similar to those that operate in the Lake District and Snowdonia.

The origins of Malham go back to AD700, to a simple community focused on the village green. Around 1100, the village was divided in two when the beck became the boundary of lands owned by the two abbeys, Fountains and Bolton. The Dissolution of the Monasteries, which removed the influence of these great estates, brought new prosperity to the dale, replacing many of the old wooden houses with stone buildings some of which still survive, along with the packhorse bridge over the beck, which dates from 1636.

'Malhamdale', however, is the name given to the upper valley of the River Aire, though the broad stream issuing from the base of the Cove is not the Aire, but Malham Beck: Aire Head is actually about half a mile south of the village.

There is no denying the simple beauty of the dale,

though, unlike others, it has no great historical associations, no baronial castles. If you come to Malhamdale it is for the landscape, and that has been very much fashioned by two major fault lines. The Mid-Craven and North Craven faults together produce a diversity of underlying rock that sustains an almost bewildering variety of plant species from the exquisite mountain pansy to the nationally rare Jacob's Ladder, from the more common foxglove to the nodding heads of cotton grass. It is this accident of nature that is the dale's most outstanding characteristic.

The River Aire, however, does not flow for long through the pleasing dale, for it is soon waylaid by a string of industrial towns to become one of the saddest rivers in the country. But it was the river that probably guided the first settlers into Malhamdale, bringing Anglo-Saxons from the east in the 6th century: there is no evidence that the Romans settled here. Where the Saxons settled they left their place names: Malham itself, Hanlith and Airton. Later came the Danes, who used '-thorpe' and '-by', instead of the Angles' '-tun' and '-ham', to tell us where they had been.

But the scenery around and above the dale is as good as anything in the Dales, and it has been the inspiration of many, including John Ruskin, and Charles Kingsley, who wrote part of *The Water Babies* while a guest of millionaire Walter Morrison at Malham Tarn House. Charles Darwin, too, was here, and found the peaceful, 'romantic' setting conducive to his studies. Indeed, as Harry Scott commented: "There can be few places so quiet and peaceful with its warm hills and pleasant streams".

It is into this splendid setting that the walks that follow will guide you, from conventional excursions to see Gordale and Malham Cove to fine moorland rambles across ancient Mastiles Lane and the old 'market' road to neighbouring Settle. Beyond the southern edge of Malhamdale proper, two walks take you out onto the wilderness of Embsay Moor and along the fine ridge of Cracoe Fell, and allow an investigation of countryside that is less well explored.

# 21 Janet's Foss and Gordale

*This is a deservedly popular walk linking four of the area's most spectacular sites — the Janet's Foss waterfall, Gordale Scar, Malham Tarn and Malham Cove. The scenery is magnificent, and the ascent of Gordale Scar far less problematic than might be supposed.*

**Distance:** 5½ miles /9km
**Height gain:** 605ft/185m
**Walking time:** 3-4 hours
**Type of walk:** *Good paths; some scrambling in Gordale*
**Start/Finish:** *Malham village car park.* GR900627

Leave the car park and turn left in front of the National Park Centre, and, just after passing the Methodist Chapel, cross the road and look for a clapper bridge spanning Malham Beck. Over the bridge turn right and follow a surfaced pathway across fields to two gates side by side. Here, turn left on a pathway, crossing a stile near a barn. Follow the on-going path through a succession of gates and stiles to enter the National Trust's Malham Tarn Estate at Janet's Foss.

The path continues through woodland to the fall,

its wooded banks in spring and summer cloaked with wild garlic, dog's mercury, herb robert, red campion and ferns.

*The pool and stream below the falls is now a popular spot with dippers, but it was once one of three local sheep washes. Sheep were washed before shearing in late June, as a better price was paid for a clean fleece. Washing also encouraged the growth of new wool, which lifts the fleece from the skin. Sheep used to be driven into the pool to be washed by men standing up to their chests in water; the day was also one of great social occasion.*

*Janet's Foss was bought by the National Trust in 1982. According to local legend, the queen of the fairies, Jennet, lives in a cave behind the fall.*

Ascend the rocky path to the left of the falls to a gate at a lane. Turn right, going past a ruined barn, and walk down the lane to Gordale Bridge. Beyond the bridge keep on as far as a gate on the left, giving access to a track running through a campsite.

*The name 'Gordale' is Norse in origin, 'gore' or 'geir' being an angular piece of land: 'dalr' means 'a valley'. For many centuries the Augustinian canons of Bolton Priory owned Gordale. Traces of foundations close to the path mark the site of a building where they are said to have held their manorial court.*

Go through the gate and follow a broad track into the gaping maw of Gordale. The path eventually wings round into the inner sanctum of Gordale, facing you with the spectacle of seriously overhanging cliffs and a double waterfall — the upper fall spills through a hole in the rock wall above, and the lower is divided by a great wedge of a rock known as tufa, a porous rock formed as a deposit by springs or streams.

Keep to the right-hand side as you walk towards the falls until you are close below the first fall. The rocks are often slippery, so take care as you paddle across the shallow stream-bed to the base of the tufa, and then climb it. There are ample, large hand- and footholds, though small folk may have a little leg stretching to do.

At the top of the tufa, step across a small stream to gain a rocky pathway, soon ascending as a flight of steps below the left-hand rock wall. The stairway leads out of the ravine onto a splendid grass and limestone ridge overlooking the course of Gordale Beck. A little more climbing leads to a through stile where virtually all the ascent finishes. Cross the stile and go forward on close-cropped turf between the limestone outcrops of Malham Lings.

Aim for a large cairn on the skyline ahead. As you draw level with it, two more come into view and give you the general direction to follow across a featureless landscape to meet a wall and lane at a stile.

Turn right, along the lane, continuing until it bends left, and there leave it, going forward on a rough-surfaced track, heading for a stand of trees. Along

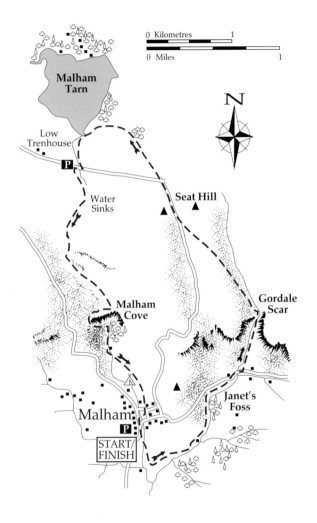

Malham Tarn

Low
Trenhouse

**P**

Water
Sinks

**Seat Hill**

0 Kilometres 1

0 Miles 1

N

**Malham
Cove**

**Gordale
Scar**

**Janet's
Foss**

**Malham**

**P**

START/
FINISH

the track a number of single trees stand protected by circular walls. After the third of these leave the track, crossing open ground on the left (no path), and aiming for the left-hand edge of a small woodland overlooking Malham Tarn.

*Malham Tarn is also owned by the National Trust, though it was originally granted to the monks of Fountains Abbey. It was later described by Charles Kingsley as a scene in his book 'The Water Babies' (1863).*

On approaching the tarn, bear left on the southbound Pennine Way, which will now be used almost all of the way back to Malham. Beyond the tarn outflow, keep forward on an obvious path to rejoin the lane left earlier.

At the lane turn right for 100yds/m to a footpath sign on the left. Leave the lane here, through a gate, and when the ensuing path forks a short way on, branch left and keep on to an area known as Water Sinks, where the shallow stream literally disappears underground. At Water Sinks ignore a stile, and keep forward with a wall on the left, heading towards the Dry Valley.

The broad grassy track gives way to a narrow rocky path which eventually swings round above a dry waterfall to the head of Watlowes, an impressive ravine formed during and just after the last Ice Age by river torrents when the underground passage ways, for which the landscape is renowned, were still filled with ice.

At a stile swing sharply left and descend into Watlowes, passing the base of the dry waterfall. The on-going path runs on easily to reach the top of Malham Cove. Here, bear right to cross a large expanse of limestone pavement, the left-hand edge of which gives a most spectacular view of the cove, but one not to be sought out by anyone suffering from vertigo or who might be unsteady on slippery rock.

Cross the limestone pavement, one of the most renowned expanses in Britain, and on the far side locate two stiles across a wall on the left. Beyond, a constructed stairway descends to the base of the cove. At the bottom, branch right to continue the walk, or go left to the very base of these towering cliffs, often festooned with the ropes of rock climbers.

*The cove is a massive white limestone cliff some 240ft (73m) high, curving round almost in a semicircle. From its base a broad stream squeezes out from a narrow gap; this water has been proven to have originated at a water sink in the vicinity of an old smelt chimney on the moors. At the end of the last Ice Age Malham Tarn was twice its present size, and its outflow filled the valley of Watlowes above and plunged over the cove in a massive waterfall. The last known waterfall over the Cove was at the beginning of the 19th century.*

Leave the cove on a surfaced path, but only as far as a clapper, or slab, bridge which allows you to cross Malham Beck.

*Clapper bridges are a fairly common means of crossing small streams throughout the Dales and the north Pennines, and occur in many other places throughout Britain.*

Cross the bridge and, through a gate, bear right, climbing a little to a small grassy ledge, heading past a ruined barn to a ladder stile in the distance.

Over the stile a clear path leads on between ancient, and less ancient walls to the youth hostel. A short way on, the path, now a substantial track, meets the road near the Listers Arms pub and Malham cafe. Turn right to cross the village bridge, and then go left along the road to return to the car park.

# 22 Malham Cove

*In addition to visiting the ever-popular Malham Cove, this brief walk climbs onto the limestone pavement above and then cuts across country towards Gordale, before returning past Janet's Foss.*

**Distance:** *3 miles/5km*
**Height gain***: 445ft /135m*
**Walking time:** *2-3 hours*
**Type of walk:** *On good*
*paths throughout, but slippery on limestone when wet.*
**Start/Finish:** *Malham car park. GR900627*

*The popularity of Malham is such that you are unlikely ever to have the place to yourself, even in the depths of winter. The cliffs of the cove are a playground for rock climbers, and many a contented hour can be spent watching their antics.*

The walk begins from the car park in the village and turns left towards its centre. Go right, over the village bridge, and shortly turn left onto the narrow lane that leads past the youth hostel. This soon becomes a narrow walled track, rising above the valley as it heads towards the cliffs of the cove. The route is straightforward and eventually, after a final ladder stile, brings you out into a small sloping pasture. Bear left to the bottom of this where you can leave the pasture and cross a clapper bridge spanning the beck that flows from the foot of the cove.

Turn right on the main cove path, and when this forks, branch left to climb a few hundred steps to a couple of stiles crossing a wall at the top of the cove. Over the wall, turn right to cross the limestone pavement for which Malham is internationally famous. Take great care crossing this at all times, and especially if it is wet. Cross it at a safe distance from the lip of the cove: many walkers head to the edge of the cliffs, and you can do likewise, but there is nothing between you and eternity if you go too far.

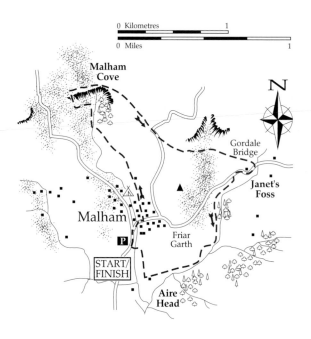

Once across the limestone you reach the dry valley that once, thousands of years ago, accommodated Malham's waterfall. Here the Pennine Way turns left to head for Malham Tarn, but you should cross the shallow valley to a stile and gate on the other side. Beyond this climb a little, heading south-east, to a wall corner on what used to be the original line of the Pennine Way. From the wall corner continue in the same direction, initially above the wall, and then descending gently to a stile giving onto a narrow lane (Malham Rakes). By turning right here you can effect a speedy return to Malham.

Otherwise, cross the lane to another stile, and keep on a south-easterly course to run alongside another wall, with steeper ground rising on your left. The wall guides you to a stile at which you can drop into a sloping pasture, descending easily on a grassy track to reach Gordale Bridge.

As you come out onto the road at Gordale Bridge (where there is often an ice cream van), turn right and walk along the road until you can leave it, on the left, to head for Janet's Foss. Again, if you omit this turning, the road will take you quickly back to the village.

The path through the woods that flank Janet's Foss is never in doubt, and steers you unerringly out of the woodland and along the edge of farm fields to a barn, soon after which you rejoin the Pennine Way, at a couple of gates. Turn right here and follow a field edge path all the way back to Malham.

# 23 Airton and Kirkby Malham

*It is difficult, if not impossible, to find scenery in Malhamdale that is not exquisite. Most walks from Malham tend to head northwards in search of it; this walk does the opposite, using the Pennine Way to go southwards to the peaceful village of Airton before returning along an ancient 'kirk' road via Kirkby Malham.*

**Distance:** *5 miles/8km*
**Height gain:** *330ft/100m*
**Walking time:** *3-3½ hours*
**Type of walk:** *Easy riverside walking to begin, followed by a little road walking before returning riverside from Kirkby Malham*
**Start/Finish:** *Malham car park. GR900627*

Start from the car park in Malham and walk towards the centre of the village, soon bearing right over a clapper bridge to pick up the southbound Pennine Way on the other side of Malham Beck. Follow the surfaced path beside the beck to two gates side by side, near a barn. Here leave the surfaced path and head across the next field on a grassy path.

About half a mile (1km) south of Malham, the route

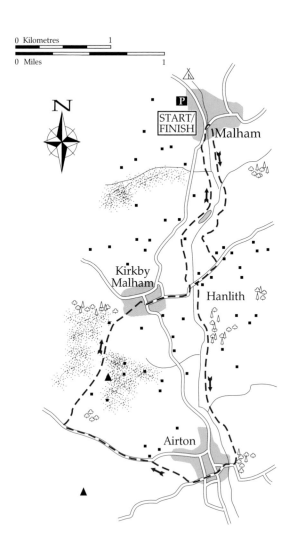

START/FINISH

P

Malham

Kirkby Malham

Hanlith

Airton

0  Kilometres                    1

0  Miles                         1

N

climbs to a stile above the River Aire, which, at Aire Head, emerges from a subterranean passageway. The way crosses a grassy slope high above the river, moving away slightly after a couple of stiles as it rounds the corner of a wall and heads across a grassy pasture to two low waymarks in mid-field which guide you towards the lane at Hanlith. After the second waymark, head for a metal gate, beyond which the path finally runs down to join a lane at a low gate.

Keep descending until you reach Hanlith Bridge, and there leave the lane, on the left, through a small gap in the bridge wall (still on the Pennine Way). A grassy path now accompanies the river for most of the way, but at one point, as the river makes a genteel loop, the path takes a more direct course to rejoin it a short way further on. At a couple of gates the route enters an important nesting area for wading birds — notably oystercatcher, curlew and redshank. Take particular care here during the breeding season not to cause disturbance.

There comes a point when two footbridges not far apart offer the potential for confusion. Take that on the left, then go through a gated gap stile before continuing on a grassy path across another open pasture. Near a derelict building you rejoin the river briefly, with the rooftops of Airton now in view to the right.

Follow an obvious path across a field to a through stile and gate. Beyond the stile, the path crosses another field to come into Airton at Airton Bridge. On the right as you reach the village there is a fine old mill building.

Turn right over the bridge and ascend past Ellis Cottage and the village green with its squatter's cottage.

*Jessica Lofthouse, in her book* Countrygoer in the Dales, *described the houses round the village green in Airton as "comely, all in harmony and mostly three centuries old". One, Ellis Cottage, was occupied by William Ellis, a linen weaver like many of his neighbours, but who became a fervent member of the Society of Friends, and travelled far afield, often as distant as America, leaving behind his house (built in 1696) and land, on the understanding that "whosoever rented the premises should willingly entertain such teachers as might be called of God and by Him sent abroad to preach the Gospel in the free dispensation thereof". Essentially this meant free board and lodgings. Nor did it end there, for Ellis also took account of the vagaries of the Yorkshire weather by providing six large coats and six women's hoods for the use of anyone caught in foul conditions.*

At a crossroads go forward on the Otterburn road. Follow this for 300yds/m and then leave it, on the right, just after Garris Lodge. At a signposted bridleway (for Scosthrop), go through two gates close together, and follow a field edge path to another gate at the end of a wall. Keep forward, following the line of an old field boundary, of which only a few ash trees remain. Go through another gate to the left of a barn (with the inscription ET 1862), and on to reach Scosthrop Lane.

Turn left and follow the lane for about half a mile/ 1km, climbing steadily, but starting to descend and rise again before leaving the road on the right over a through stile (signposted for Kirkby Malham). Across the stile ascend the field margin beside a wall. When some old quarries come into view start aiming for the left-hand edge of woodland on the skyline ahead, and this will bring you to a through stile near the top of Warber Hill.

Beyond the stile go forward, still with a wall on the right. Keep on down the field, ignoring a stile on the right, and finally leaving the field at a small gate (Kirk Gait) on the right. Go down to cross a stream-bed, and heed the direction of a nearby signpost as you cross the next field, moving away from a right-hand wall on an indistinct path, though this does not guide you to the stile in a field corner, at a junction between a wall and fence. Here you get a sudden view of Kirkby Malham, just a short way ahead now.

Cross the stile and the immediate track, and go down the next field beside woodland, aiming for the church tower ahead. Cross another stile and go down the next field, gradually bearing right to a through stile. A brief pasture crossing leads to a garlicky woodland, through which a rough-stepped path leads down to the lane by the church. Turn right, going towards the Victoria Inn.

*There seems to be little that is modern in Kirkby Malham, almost as if nothing has changed since the days when the fraternities of Fountains Abbey and Bolton Priory held extensive tracts of land around here. They rebuilt the church, dedicated to St Michael the Archangel, in the 15th century, in the Perpendicular style, on a site thought to have been occupied by a Danish church. Closer investigation, however, and a little judicious study of old accounts of village life here, tells that although the stocks remain, the old ducking stool, used to determine (in a brutal and often terminal way) whether the victim had witchly proclivities, is missing. There was a time, too, when the churchwardens used to dispense ale, presumably as an antidote to the sermons, but now the local pub must press on without this age-old assistance to its cause.*

*Oliver Cromwell is known to have stayed with General Lambert at nearby Calton Hall, and is said to have added his name to the register of two couples getting married in the church, a demonstration by the couples, we are left to assume, of contemporary one-upmanship. There is, however, a goodly measure of doubt about this.*

*But it is with a more recent worthy that Kirkby Malham identifies, for it was here that John Dower lived during the last war. While living here, he was commissioned to prepare a report on national parks in England and Wales, which was published in 1945, and augured the development of national parks. The offices of the Countryside Commission in Cheltenham were named in his memory.*

At the crossroads by the Victoria Inn go forward for

Hanlith, noting some cottages with interesting dates (1637 and 1667). Keep on down the lane to Hanlith Bridge, but do not cross the bridge, going instead left on a riverside path, along a surfaced lane beside the Aire. The lane leads to Scalegill Mill (now holiday homes), and there go through a gate to the left of the buildings.

*There has been activity here since the 11th century when it was mentioned in the Domesday Book. Originally the site of a corn mill, the existing buildings were erected in 1795 for spinning cotton, making it the major employer in Kirkby Malham. The waterwheel was removed in 1924, when water turbines were installed, which remained in use until the early 1990s.*

Go round the old mill before continuing beside a constructed channel which fed the mill wheel. As you head for Malham, first Gordale Scar and then the Cove come into view in the distance.

Grassy paths now lead on through fields to the southern edge of the village, the way onward marked by stiles of one form or another.

# 24 Malham to Settle

*Henry Bracton, a 13th-century English lawyer, considered, among other things, that markets in order to justify themselves should be no closer than the distance that could be travelled in a day, then considered to be 20 miles. Of course, he concluded, it would be necessary to spend some of that day at the market, and in returning home. So he revised his calculations and stipulated that the maximum range for a market journey would be a third of 20 miles, or, as he put it, "six miles and a half and the third part of a half". When this is applied to the known market towns of the Yorkshire Dales, it can be seen that there are few places outside a seven-mile radius; and such is the relationship between Malham and Settle, communities that are linked in this linear walk by a traditional "market" route.*

| | |
|---|---|
| **Distance:** 5½ miles/9km | *walking on a clear path throughout* |
| **Height gain:** 1,035 ft /315m | **Start:** *Malham GR900627* |
| **Walking time:** 3 hours | **Finish:** *Settle. GR818637* |
| **Type of walk:** *Easy* | |

*Although life in the Middle Ages tended to be very parochial — based on manors and villages, monasteries and castle-life — from the 13th century there developed greater mobility, a greater willingness to travel further afield, for example to exchange excess farm produce and the range of manufactured goods that were the trademark* of many rural communities. Markets therefore often evolved around the periphery of settled areas, where upland farming met the arable farming of the lowlands, where turnpikes and other major lines of communication had developed. And again it is easy to see how Malham with, as Jessica Lofthouse puts it *"an atmosphere all its own, cradling peace"*, set in a seclusion that even today necessitates travelling six or so miles to Gargrave to stock up on provisions, needed to develop its links with Settle which stood on one of the old Yorkshire highways.

The pedestrian route between Malham and Settle is today a delightful and in places stunning walk, but one that needs a little pre-planning. It is not so long that you couldn't simply turn round and walk back, but here the walk is presented as a linear walk with the express intention, in this age of increasing support for the use of public transport, of encouraging walkers to use the Keighley and District bus service that links Settle with Malham, so enabling a relaxed return to the starting point.

Walk up into the centre of the village, as if heading for Malham Cove. Near a telephone box on the right, leave the road for a short while and go through a gate to follow a wooded path beside Malham Beck which soon enough returns you to the road. Cross the road and go up a bridleway (signposted) opposite. This rises to a T-junction, and here go left for about 40yds/m, before bearing right on a broad, ascending, rough-surfaced track, Long Lane. Follow the track, and when it forks just after the Malham Water Treatment Works building, branch right. The rough surfacing ends after a while, but the track continues as a pleasant green lane between walls to a gate. From it there are fine views, especially eastwards across wall-patterned fields, while the sheer cliff face of Malham Cove is unmistakable.

Beyond the gate the walls end, so continue on an obvious green path until you reach the Malham road at a bend. Walk up the road for about 400yds/m, and then leave it at a gate on the left (signposted: Settle 4m). After about 100yds/m of rising track, bear right (look for a low waymark post) and follow the on-going track as it winds through low limestone outcrops. When the track forks again a short way on, branch left, still climbing. The gradient soon eases and the track becomes grassy and leads onwards to Fair Sleets Gate, just below Pikedaw Hill, marked by a large cairn. All is green tranquillity now, but this area was once the centre of a calamine- and copper-mining industry owned by Lord Ribblesdale.

As you pass to the north of Pikedaw Hill the track starts to climb again before easing as it presses on towards a gate in a wall north of Kirkby Fell. Beside the track in spring and summer grow mountain pansies and saxifrage, the white flowers of the latter often in such profusion that they form a delicate blanket, like a light dusting of snow.

Between Kirkby Fell and Rye Loaf Hill you reach the highest point of the crossing (510m), the path finally starting to descend as you draw level with Rye Loaf Hill. North of the Hill, when the descending grassy path forks, branch left,

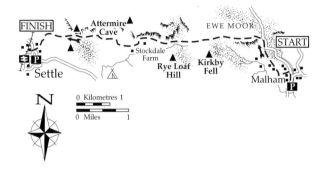

following a clear path onwards towards the buildings of Stockdale Farm ahead.

Just after passing north of Stockdale Farm, at a gate you meet surfaced Stockdale Lane, the farm access. Head down the lane, below the bright limestone outcrops of Settle Scar. As Stockdale Lane bends sharply left, leave it on the right through a metal gate, and turn immediately left beside a wall, heading now for the conspicuous crags of Attermire Scar.

Gradually drift away from the wall to a gate in a lateral wall, and through this branch left to the bottom left-hand corner of a pasture. The path continues to run along below the crags and on to reach a wall gap beyond which it goes forward through two pastures as a green path with a wall on the left-hand side. Just as you pass through the next wall, with a low cave nearby, the grassy track moves away from the wall, to the right.

131

As you finally clear the end of the crags, at an old gateway, with the on-going grassy path descending half-right towards a distant quarry, so the unmistakable profile of Ingleborough comes into view.

Soon, the grey roofs of Settle appear in the valley below, and as they do, so the path starts to descend more steeply and bears left to reach a walled track. When the descending track meets a surfaced lane keep forward and follow lanes down into Market Square in Settle.

# 25 Mastiles Lane and Bordley

*Although beginning in the ever popular Malham village, this walk soon finds its way into less well populated areas around the isolated and widespread community that flanks Bordley Beck and its numerous tributaries. There's a nip in the air up here on an autumn day.*

| | |
|---|---|
| **Distance:** *11 miles / 17.5km* | *walking, but quite exposed and isolated across the moors* |
| **Height gain:** *1,395ft/425m* | **Start/Finish:** *Malham village car park GR900627* |
| **Walking time:** *5 hours* | |
| **Type of walk:** *Easy* | |

Leave the car park and go left into the village, crossing the bridge and going past the Listers Arms and up past cottages. Turn left on the lane signposted to Malham Tarn (Malham Rakes), and follow it as it climbs steadily, as far as a rocky knoll on the skyline ahead and to the left.

After a couple of steeper sections the lane bends sharply right. Here leave the lane at a stile on the left, and follow a path going forward towards the top of Malham Cove. Near a wall corner the path forks, with the left-hand path descending to the valley above the cove, and the right-hand path, the way to go, heading along the former course of the Pennine Way on an old monastic track, known as Trougate, through splendid limestone outcrops to reach a road not far from Malham Tarn. Turn right alongside the road until you can leave it, going forward through Street Gate and onto Mastiles Lane.

*Mastiles Lane is one of the best known monastic roads in northern England, though the name itself only applies to the section that crosses Malham Moor to the former Cistercian grange at Kilnsey. The route, however, continues westwards into Lakeland to Fountains Abbey estates there. 'Mastiles' is a fairly recent name for the road; its former name was Strete Gate, an association, no doubt, with the nearby Roman marching camp.*

The track soon dips to cross a stream before climbing again to go through the site of the Roman camp. Further on, Mastiles Lane becomes enclosed by walls. At a gate the track forks, Mastiles Lane, which here ceases to be enclosed by walls on both sides and continues as a close-cropped green sward, goes left (signposted to Kilnsey), while a bridleway branches right. Here go left, staying with Mastiles Lane for a while longer, until, after a short descent, the track comes down to Mastiles Gate, beyond which it continues as a walled track once more.

Don't go through the gate, but turn right on a bridleway with a wall on your left. The bridleway, which is grassy throughout, eventually runs on to meet a rough-surfaced track. Cross the track, and go through a metal gate opposite, on a bridleway signposted to Bordley.

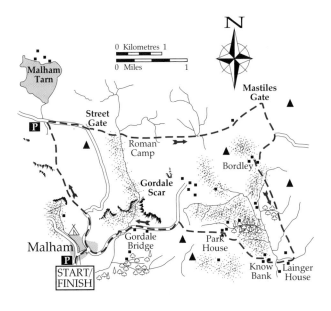

As you come down to Bordley House Farm, turn left in front of the farmhouse, on a bridleway (signposted to Boss Moor), and passing through three gates before following the on-going track beside a wall.

The path bends down to cross a stream, goes through a gate, and climbs a little to another gate, before pressing on along the top edge of a small plantation. Keep on across the top of a track ascending from Bordley Hall in the valley below, towards Wood Gill Plantation. Keep going down the lane until you pass High Lainger House, and come to a telephone box. Cross a stream here, and then turn right on footpath (signposted to Know Bank Farm).

Follow the track up to the farm, and just as you pass through the farmyard gate, bear left through another gate on a footpath (signposted to Malham), following a rough track between walls to reach a large open pasture. Go forward with a fence on your left, and later a wall, to a gate. Beyond the gate keep forward along the line of a grubbed-out hedgerow. As you reach a more open area of upland pasture start moving across to the right on a broad green track generally heading towards a wall on the right, and higher up head for a gate in a wall corner. Keep going forward beside the wall. As you go over the field look for a bend in the wall, in the middle of which there is a stone through stile. Cross the stile and go over the next field to a gate.

Through the gate head for the buildings of Park House Farm on a clear track across a field. Go forward and to the left of the main farm building and through a metal gate, and then onto the right-hand of three gates. Go up the field beyond following the right-hand wall to a gap stile in a lateral wall ahead. Keep on along a wall and when this turns right keep going in much the same direction on a narrow path heading for a wall corner beyond a widespread group of larch. Over a through stile keep forward with a wall on your right to another stile/gate not far ahead. Through the gate cross open pasture in the same direction, and soon you will see another gap stile in a wall. Head for this. It gives onto a walled track. Turn right and follow it round and down to Hawthorn Lane.

Now all that remains is to go left, down Hawthorn Lane below the steep fellside of Cross Field Knotts to cross Gordale Bridge, and then on down Gordale Lane back into Malham.

# 26 Embsay Moor

*The moors north of Embsay and Eastby have long been water catchment areas, but they are open to walkers who go in search of solitude and peace. For much of the year, only the sound of moorland birds — curlew, grouse, meadow pipit, skylark and snipe — rises above the wild whisper of wind and water. On a warm summer's day it is easy to leave troubles behind and to relax in a simple landscape.*

**Distance:** *6 miles/10km*
**Height gain:** *1,065ft/325m*
**Walking time:** *3-4 hours*

**Type of walk:** *A wild moorland walk on good tracks throughout*
**Start/Finish:** *Village car park. GR009538*

The walk, which circles anticlockwise onto the moors, starts from the small, attractive village of Embsay.

Go through a gate at the rear of the village car park and bear right across a small enclosure to a through stile in a wall corner. A narrow path ensues, leading to another stile and a field, across which a grassy path cuts a swathe to a gate on the Eastby road. Turn left and go past the church of St Mary the Virgin, immediately after which leave the road, on the right, along a surfaced path across two fields, at the end of which a short path leads to the road once more. Turn right, towards the hamlet of Eastby for about 300yds/m, leaving the road at a footpath on the left immediately after Croft House (signposted for Eastby Moor).

Go past a few houses to cross a stile at the foot of a sunken green lane. The lower section of the lane is tree-lined, then at another stile breaks free of its cover and continues rising onto the edge of Embsay Moor. A series of stiles guides you on to reach the start of access land at Eastby Gate.

From the last stile walk northwards on a narrow trod through rushes, aiming for the first of a line of shooting butts. Swing right, following the line of butts until, after butt number 10, Lower Barden Reservoir comes into view, set against the backdrop of Barden Fell. Soon the track begins to descend, and reaches a bridleway at the top of Hutchen Gill. Turn left, rising steadily, pass butt number 12, and then branch right on a clear grassy track — look for a sign prohibiting dogs and cyclists. After loping across the slopes of Embsay Moor the track finally reaches Upper Barden Reservoir.

*To the north-west the memorial on Cracoe Fell commands attention, while the waters of, and the grounds surrounding, the reservoir are often host to cacophonous assemblies of black-headed gulls.*

As you reach the reservoir the track branches. Go left (signposted: Eastby) and snake easily back up onto Embsay Moor. When the track meets another,

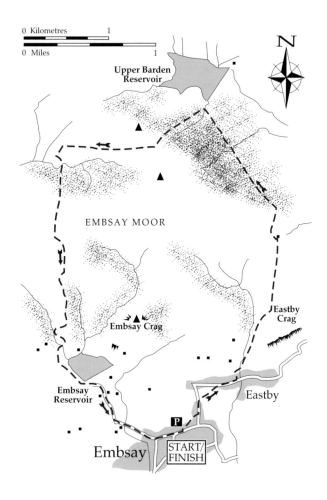

0 Kilometres 1

0 Miles 1

N

Upper Barden
Reservoir

EMBSAY MOOR

Embsay Crag

Eastby
Crag

Embsay
Reservoir

Eastby

P

START/
FINISH

Embsay

branch right to a signpost, and then keep forward for Rylstone. Further on (about half a mile/1km), the track forks, with a bridleway branching right. Go left here past two shelters and follow a track across the moor, heading roughly southwards.

Once the track has started to descend towards Embsay Moor Reservoir, the pronounced track ends, and a narrow footpath takes over, continuing in the same direction.

As you come down to the edge of the reservoir, go right to a stile/gate and turn left to pass beside the reservoir, finally feeding onto a lane that runs down to Embsay. Follow the road as it leads into the northern edge of the village, going past the Elm Tree Inn to reach the car park a short distance further on.

# 27 Cracoe Fell

*A brief stretch of rough going on the descent is the only price you pay for a splendid circuit high above the villages of Rylstone and Cracoe, which visits two important monuments. One commemorates Cracoe's war dead; the other is the conspicuous cross on Rylstone Fell.*

| | |
|---|---|
| **Distance:** *4¼ miles/7km* | *rough descent from Cracoe* |
| **Height gain:** *1,000ft* | *Fell to Fell Lane, which is* |
| */305m* | *trackless.* |
| **Walking time:** *4 hours* | **Start/Finish:** *Rylstone* |
| **Type of walk:** *Generally* | *church. GR972588* |
| *on good paths, except for a* | *Limited parking* |

*Rylstone is a delightful village in a splendid setting on one of the oldest routes northwards from Skipton to Wharfedale. Its church, standing away from the road, occupies one of the finest positions of any church in the Dales. This land was under the control of the Nortons, a powerful family invariably quarrelling with the neighbouring Cliffords over deer or cattle. There is a ruined tower on Rylstone Fell, built by Richard Norton, a leader in the Pilgrimage of Grace, who subsequently forfeited his estates to the Cliffords.*

*Wordsworth's poem, The White Doe of Rylstone, tells the legend that a son of the family, Francis, not implicated in the rebellion, was murdered near Bolton. His sister, Emily, was often then seen taking her pet white doe to*

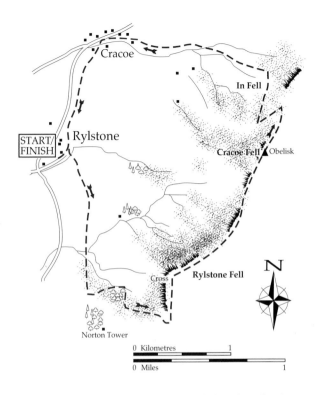

*her brother's grave on Sundays, a habit that the doe continued after Emily's death.*

At the top of the lane leading to St Peter's Church in Rylstone, turn right on a footpath for Sandy Beck Bar. A short way on, at a gate, go through a gated stile and follow the ensuing field margin forward to another stile giving into a narrow strip of woodland. Follow the on-going path beside a wall until another gated stile gives access to a large pasture. Head across this, aiming to the right of a small group of trees, and when a vehicle track comes into view ahead and right, head for it, finally reaching it over two ladder stiles.

Walk up a track for about 100yds/m, and then go left through a field gate onto a vehicle track that ascends across Countryside Stewardship Access Land, going left of a small plantation before rising steadily to a gate. Rylstone Cross appears on the skyline to the left.

Stay with the ascending track as far as a dilapidated wall on the edge of the bleak open moorland of Out Fell (Rylstone Fell). Here turn left and follow the wall passing, and visiting, Rylstone Cross (reconstructed in 1995). Press on along the top of the fell to the towering war memorial on Watt Crag, the highest point of Cracoe Fell.

As you approach the top of the fell, the accompanying wall bends to the left, but the path keeps on in the same direction to a ladder stile that allows you over the wall, and so to the memorial.

The easiest return is to retrace your steps, but, though largely trackless, to continue instead to the hamlet of Cracoe allows you to complete a pleasant circuit.

From the memorial head north for about 600yds/m until the ground starts to steepen. A narrow path through rough upland pasture guides you to a shallow sunken way that gradually changes direction, heading north-west, before finally petering out. Continue to descend in the same north-westerly direction until the sheep pens at the head of Fell Lane come into view. Once located, head for them as directly as possible.

A gate on the right of the pens gives access to them, and then three more gates bring you to Fell Lane. Follow the lane as it descends through pleasant farming landscapes to reach the edge of Cracoe. Turn left in front of cottages and along a lane opposite a large information panel. Follow the lane — it later becomes a narrow track — almost to reach the B6265. But, just as you approach the B-road, turn left on Chapel Lane, a walled bridleway that contours across the bottom of pastures towards Rylstone.

When the track bends right, go left through a gate and along the edge of a field containing disused fish ponds that may well have served the nearby Manor House.

By keeping right, a gate is reached adjacent to Manor House Farm. Through this the church is soon reached.

# DENTDALE AND THE HOWGILLS

From the moment you enter Dentdale at Dent Head you become aware that here is something special. In its upper reaches the river flows over long flat stretches of limestone bedrock, from which it has shaped its own miniature cascades that are a lively companion in all but the driest conditions.

This, not far from Ribblehead, is wild, mountain country, isolated from the other dales, formerly part of the West Riding of Yorkshire, but now part of Cumbria. As if underscoring the isolation, Dentdale perches its station (one of few among the dales) high on a shelf-like ledge on Great Knoutberry Hill, a massive mound of a fell that effectively seals the eastern end of the valley.

On the northern flank rises the whaleback ridge of Aye Gill Pike and Rise Hill, devoid of rights of way and ready for open access legislation that at last would allow walkers to see Dentdale from a different angle. That said, there are two excellent tracks to the south — the Occupation Road, which crosses Crag Hill and Great Combe, and the Craven Way, which rounds the northern end of Whernside, linking Dentdale with Ribblehead. Both these ancient tracks are used in the walks that follow.

Following the Wars of the Roses, Dentdale was in

the hands of owner-farmers, 'Four and Twenty' of whom constituted a form of local government that dates from 1429. This practice continued until the late 19th century when parish councils took over most of their functions. The '24' was a version of the parish vestry found elsewhere, but constituted in a manner which appears to be a relic of Norse settlement — other 24s occurred in a number of Norse-settled areas, though Dent may well be the only place where it has survived. The 24 consisted of men who represented the longest-established and more prosperous families, vacancies among them being filled by nomination — usually the eldest son or nearest kinsman of the member who had died. Today the 24 of Dent exists as a registered charity meeting at least once a year.

It was wool that made Dent. Many of the natural stone-built houses in the main, cobbled street of Dent used to have first-floor galleries, where 'the terrible knitters i' Dent' (described by Robert Southey in his miscellany *The Doctor*), who formed a thriving cottage industry, would sit knitting simple garments from which Dentdale ultimately derived its share of fame. Everyone, it seemed, young and old alike, knitted.

In 1800, with a population a little under 2000, Dent was very much a self-contained settlement, with many trades flourishing, including marble quarrying, horse-breeding and coal mining. Now only the cobbled streets, the church and a few plaques and monuments tell of those distant times.

At the other end of the dale, Sedbergh, in spite of its administrative connections with Cumbria, remains one of the largest towns in the Yorkshire Dales National Park, and is the main western gateway to the Dales.

The Turnpike Acts of 1761 brought improvements to the Askrigg-Kendal and Lancaster-Kirkby Stephen roads, both of which pass through Sedbergh, and these improvements made the town more accessible for commercial routes across the Pennines. There followed a time of industrial growth as the domestic knitting trade was augmented by a cotton industry based on mills at Birks, Howgill and Millthrop. As a result, Sedbergh grew at the expense of Dent, which hitherto had been the more important township.

Above the town rise the rounded hills of the Howgills, a popular place with walkers and lovers of wide, open spaces.

The Howgills are free range country, where the fells offer excellent long walks on velvet turf, untamed by walls or fences; fells that rise steeply from glaciated valleys, their sides creased into deep, shady gullies, and, for the most part, their sweeping graceful lines unbroken by outcrops of the underlying rock.

Were it not for the roads and railway line that muscle their way through the Lune gorge, the Howgills would be largely unknown territory for the hill-walking fraternity, being neither Dales nor

North Pennines, nor having a strong grip on Lakeland. Even so, they are still relatively little known, a remarkable featureless wilderness of rolling fells, where black-faced Rough Fell sheep and wild fell ponies thrive on the dry fellsides; a place of charm and beauty.

There are few rights of way across the Howgills, and most of the walks that follow are across land where you wander by the grace of those who own the land or earn a living from it. Considerate walkers have done so for many years, and there is every reason for ensuring that no one's actions cause this delectable walking country to be prohibited to those who greatly enjoy its freedom.

# 28 Dent and the Craven Way

*Much has been written over the years about the almost legendary Settle to Carlisle railway line: this walk provides an opportunity (or an excuse) to travel on it, and to visit the delectable village of Dent. The walk begins from Dent Station and finishes at Ribblehead. Walkers arriving by train will have no trouble with the logistics; those arriving by car should leave it conveniently parked at Ribblehead, and catch the train up to Dent Station.*

**Distance:** *12 miles/19km*
**Height gain:** *1,330ft/405m*
**Walking time:** *5-6 hours*
**Type of walk:** *Generally easy; not advised in poor*
*visibility*
**Start:** *Dent Station GR764875*
**Finish:** *Ribblehead GR764791*

On leaving Dent Station turn left and walk down the road to a junction at Lea Yeat. Leave the road by a stile to gain a footpath (part of the Dales Way) on the south bank of the River Dee, and follow this to Ewegales Bridge. Turn left up a narrow road, pass Ewegales Farm and then go left through a gate into a broad, sloping pasture. Head for the farm buildings at Rivling, but keep below them and press on ahead to a stile giving access to a

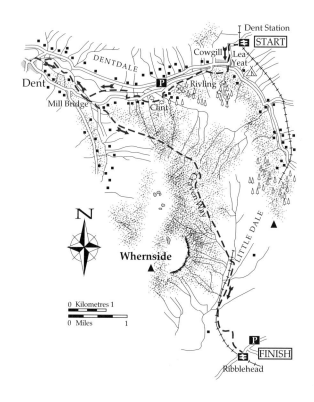

spruce plantation.

The path through the plantation is not among the best, floundering from one boggy interlude to another. As it approaches Little Town the path passes to the right of buildings. Cross an access track to a stile for more plantation, towards the end of which the path rises to meet two more stiles by means of which it escapes from the trees. It then follows the line of a wall to another access track.

Follow this access track, slightly uphill, for a short distance, and then branch right across a minor stream to another stile before racing on to meet the access to Hackergill and Coat Faw, where you get your first view of Dent ahead.

Near Coat Faw a ladder stile gives access to a small meadow on the far side of which another stile gives onto a path beneath a prominent scar. Approaching Clint, the path is deflected around the back of the buildings, and then drops to a stile and gate in a corner from which it resumes a level course. Pass West Clint and at a corner of a field leave the track for a stile, and continue past a barn and across a stream.

Just beyond the stream aim right to pass round a large barn, immediately joining the access to Laithbank Farm, and turning right to descend to a road. Go left along the road until just past a house, Tub Hole, on the left, you can turn right through a gate into a field. Go across the field to the tree-lined ravine of Lenny's Leap, passing to the right of it to rejoin the river at Nelly Bridge, a concealed footbridge spanning the river.

Over the bridge go left, down-river, and pass several stiles to reach another footbridge, Tommy Bridge, back over the Dee. Once across the bridge go right. At a second gate cross a stile on the left and leave the river once more to climb beside a wall. Keep ahead, aiming to the left of a group of trees, climbing a low hillock, and then aiming for a stile (initially unseen) near Bridge End Farm at Mill Bridge.

The on-going walk now heads for Dent, but will return to Mill Bridge for the final stage over to Ribblehead.

Cross Mill Bridge and go into trees on the right, following a path that courts Deepdale Beck as far as its confluence with the Dee. Now follow the path along the banks of the Dee until, just before Church Bridge, flood embankments divert the path left to cross a minor stream, beyond which the path goes right, continuing by stiles to Church Bridge. Dent village lies up the road to the left.

*Many of the natural stone-built houses in the main, cobbled street of Dent used to have first-floor galleries, where 'the terrible knitters i' Dent', who formed a thriving cottage industry, would sit knitting simple garments from which Dentdale ultimately derived its share of fame.*

*On one street corner, a huge fountain, carved from a block of granite, commemorates Adam Sedgwick (1785-1873), born at the Old Parsonage. He was a great Victorian geologist whose work laid the foundations for modern geological studies, and for more than 50 years he was Woodwardian Professor of Geology at Cambridge. One record does suggest, however, that at the time the professorship became vacant, Sedgwick was practically ignorant of the subject, and only on his election as professor did he begin to study it. He was later elected President of the Geological Society, President of the*

*British Association, and, in 1834, became a Canon of Norwich Cathedral. Sedgwick is buried at Trinity College, Cambridge.*

Having 'toured' Dent, retrace your steps to Mill Bridge.

When you come out on the road at Mill Bridge, turn left and go along it, rising gently, and take the first turning on the right, an ascending surfaced lane. After 300yds/m, turn left at a signpost for the Craven Way, and then 50yds/m further on, turn right to join the Great Wold, which crosses the northern end of Whernside.

The rising, walled lane leads to a ladder stile and gate beyond which a rough track continues the ascent onto the moor.

After passing a radio mast the track crosses open moorland, going forward to a wall corner. Just past this ignore the footpath to Laithbank Farm. Keep forward on a stony track with a wall on your left. High up on the moors the track collects a second wall, and continues as an enclosed lane once more. Later it breaks free of the walls and crosses open moorland, gradually becoming less distinct to the point where navigation could be a difficulty in poor visibility.

The track reaches its high point and starts to descend, first with Pen-y-ghent in view ahead and then Ingleborough and Whernside, gradually joining the Whernside path from Ribblehead.

Continue down past the aqueduct that crosses the Settle-Carlisle railway, and keep on down an obvious track to Ribblehead.

# 29 The Occupation Road and Deepdale

*High above Dentdale the so-called 'Occupation Road', an ancient highway dating from 1859, sweeps across the moorland hillsides of Great Coum and Green Hill. This walk follows its course before finally giving up the high ground for a steady descent through verdant Deepdale, and an easy return to Dent along a stretch of the Dales Way.*

**Distance:** *8 miles/13km*
**Height gain:** *1,230ft /375m*
**Walking time:** *5 hours*
**Type of walk:**
*Although on good tracks/paths throughout,* *the section across the hill moors can be bleak, and should not be contemplated in poor visibility*
**Start/Finish:** *Dent GR70487*

Start from the car park in Dent and leave it to cross the road and go up the lane signposted to the Shop on the Green. Just as you pass the village green go forward continuing uphill on a signposted bridleway for Flinter Gill. At the top of the surfaced lane, keep forward on a rising stony track. This is a former packhorse trail that climbed up to meet the Occupation Road before heading westwards across South Lord's Land into Barbondale.

The track rises steadily through the wooded Flinters Gill. At the top of the gill the track is less stony, and goes forward as a walled lane to meet the Occupation Road.

*A conveniently placed bench erected in memory of John H MacNeil is a suitable place from which to gaze across the valley to the Howgills and the low eastern outliers of the Lake District. Immediately to the west lies Barbondale and the steep slopes of Calf Top.*

When you reach the Occupation Road turn left, still on a bridleway to High Moss. Most of the track across the moor is contained by walls, but as you reach its highest point it breaks free of these for a while before curving round to go down to the road, just before which it becomes a broad walled track again.

Parts of the 'uncontained' section can be a little confusing in poor visibility, and the moors here are an inhospitable place. The track sweeps across them in a roughly southwards direction, passing below an apparently insignificant lump, Green Hill, which proves to be the highest summit in Lancashire, for the ridge above marks not only the boundary of the Yorkshire Dales National Park, but also that of Cumbria and Lancashire.

Gradually, the track changes direction, heading east, before a final cast about near High Pike. A short way on you then join the Deepdale road.

When you reach the road, turn left and go down

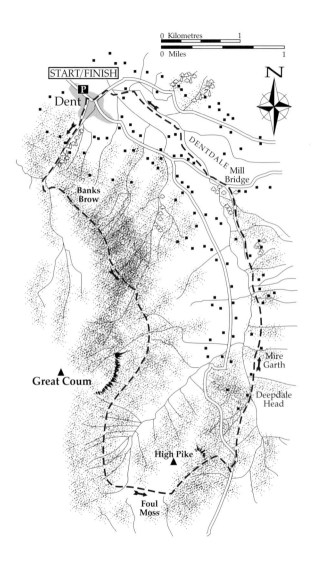

START/FINISH

Dent

DENTDALE

Mill Bridge

Banks Brow

Great Coum

Mire Garth

Deepdale Head

High Pike

Foul Moss

0 Kilometres 1

0 Miles 1

N

159

for about 300yds/m, and then leave it, on the right, at a ladder stile giving onto a footpath signposted to Mire Garth. Go steeply down rough hill pasture on a grassy path to reach a footpath signpost above Deepdale Head Farm. Continue going down along a brief grassy ridge to a ladder stile. Over the stile keep on down beside a fence.

As you meet a concrete track adjoining the farm, cross it and go down to a gate. Through the gate go to the right of buildings to cross a stream on a concrete bridge, and then through a gate turn left. Descend to pass a barn, and lower down curve round on a grassy path that rises slightly to cross a stream at a ford, and going forward to a barn from where a gap stile comes into view.

In the next field bear half right across a wall corner to a gate, and then go across the next field to Mire Garth Farm, and follow its access out to a gate. Just as you pass the farm, leave its access track and go across a field with a wall on your right to a gap stile, and then cross two more fields keeping close to a wall on the right-hand side. In the next field, keep on in the same direction aiming just to the left of a barn in the top right corner of the field, and then go into a dip to cross a stream, on the other side of which there's a ladder stile.

Beyond follow a grassy path across a field to another stream and gap stile, and then keep on to a step stile at a wall corner. Still maintaining the same direction, go down-field to a small gate, and then stay in the same direction, and when you reach a walled vehicle track, turn left (Dike Hall Lane). Go past a farm and keep on down the lane, descending to reach the valley road just south-east of Mill Bridge. Turn left to Mill Bridge.

Cross the bridge and go into trees on the right, following a path that follows Deepdale Beck to its confluence with the River Dee. Now follow the path along the banks of the Dee until, just before Church Bridge, flood embankments divert the path left to cross a minor stream, beyond which the path goes right, continuing to Church Bridge on the edge of Dent. The village centre lies up the road to the left.

*The 12th-century church of St Andrew is worth a visit. It probably came under the care of the monks at Coverham Abbey, near Middleham. Rebuilding became necessary in 1417, and more restoration followed in the 16th, 18th and 19th centuries.*

# 30 Sedbergh to Dent

*The countryside between Sedbergh and Dent has great charm and is a pleasure to walk. Much of it was formed from a massive glacial lake, and at times the meadows alongside the River Dee still flood. It is a place of lush pastures and numerous small woodlands that are a delight to explore. This walk links a series of Dentdale farms as it heads across country to Denton on the new line of the Dales Way. It then returns along the Dales Way old route.*

**Distance:** *10miles/16.5km*
**Height gain:** *130ft/40m*
**Walking time:** *4 hours*
**Type of walk:** *Easy walking on good field*
*paths and farm tracks; wet in places*
**Start/Finish:** *Loftus Hill car park, Sedbergh GR658919*

*In spite of its administrative connections with Cumbria, Sedbergh remains one of the largest towns in the Yorkshire Dales National Park, and is the main western gateway to the Dales. It is a small, stone-built town on the edge of the Howgills, and became part of Cumbria in 1974, even though it remains in the Yorkshire Dales National Park, and clearly has many 'Dales' affinities.*

*As an ancient market town Sedbergh has a charter dating from 1251, and is mentioned in the Domesday Book as among the many manors held by Earl Tostig of*

*Northumbria. Today the fame of the town rests on the laurels of its school, which is set in parkland on the edge of the town. It was founded in 1525, and has grown steadily to earn a national reputation. The old building of the school, built in 1716, is now the library, to the south-east of the church.*

The walk begins from the Loftus Hill car park, not far from the church. Turn left out of the car park and walk along the road, going past Busk Lane to continue down to cross the River Rawthey. Over the river take the first turning on the left (signposted: Millthrop), and turn right at the next junction to go through this small hamlet. As you reach the last buildings, forsake the road by branching left onto a walled track (signposted: Frostrow). Follow the track up through a gate and out onto upland pasture. After a short descent to cross a stream the on-going track forks. Here branch left up a steepening track, and soon leave it at a prominent, low rock to head for a gate to the right of a small plantation of larches.

Through the gate go beside a wall along the top edge of a pasture. Pass through a short section of walled green lane and then continue past another small woodland, mainly of sycamore and larch, to be funnelled back along an enclosed track that takes you to a gate at the edge of Gap Wood, and then on along a stony path along the woodland boundary. Beyond, you head across another field to pass Gap Farm, and set off along its access track.

Very soon, however, go left at a narrow, gated stile

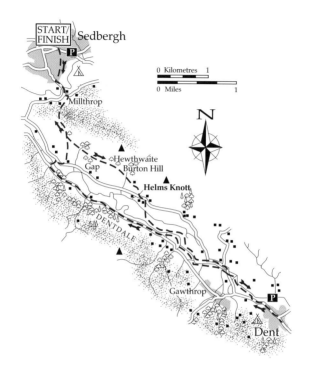

onto a signposted footpath, to cross two fields to Hewthwaite Farm. Over the farm access follow waymarks across the next pasture, and go on through a gate to Burton Hill Farm. Pass through the farmyard and out along its access road to a ladder stile on the left. Over this cross the top edge of the next field, and beyond that cross to a wall gap to keep on in the direction of Leakses Farm, which now comes into view ahead.

Follow a waymarked route through the farmyard and through a gap stile to go down steps, across an access and over a stile opposite, and then descend the sloping field beyond to the bottom left-hand corner (the top end of the field is boggy, and requires evasive tactics). Through a stile at the bottom, turn right to go out to meet a lane opposite Craggs Farm.

Turn left along the road until you reach Mire House (an attractive white cottage with a 1635 datestone), and here leave the road, turning right onto a track, and immediately branching left through two gates to follow a track across fields towards the River Dee. When the track switches sides of a hedgerow, start moving away across the corner of a field, on a grassy path, to another stile and field before reaching the river flood embankment. Turn left along this, and go past a footbridge at Ellers to continue on a path that is never far from the river, until you are forced upwards to meet a road.

Turn right and immediately pass a small memorial on the left to Lucy Elam that reads: This stone is erected by the landowners and inhabitants of Dent in grateful acknowledgement to Lucy Elam at whose sole charge this deviation road 1122 yards in length was made AD 1876 in filial love and remembrance and to fulfil the wishes of her father John Elam.

Keep on along the road to Barth Bridge, and having crossed this, go left down steps onto the Dales Way. Easy pathways now take you across the edge of fields, always close by the river, until you emerge on a road not far from Dent. Turn left along the road and walk up to the village.

For the return you retrace your steps as far as Barth Bridge, but instead of turning right over it, go forward down steps on the other side of the road, along the true left bank of the river. Between Barth Bridge and Ellers the route closely follows the river, often along the top of flood banks, and passing through a brief wooded section that can be a little awkward, especially after rain or flooding.

Eventually the path moves away from the river, and goes out to meet a road. Turn right and follow this quiet back lane for 1½ miles (2.5km) until you meet Rash Bridge. Cross the bridge and walk up to a road junction. There, turn right for about 125yds/m until you can turn left into a field on a footpath signposted for Millthrop, and walk up-field on a grassy path to a wall corner. Then continue beside the wall, up two fields to meet a walled lane used on the outward route, near the sycamore and beech woodland.

Over a through stile go left along the walled track. When this opens out and forks, branch right beside the right-hand wall. Go through the gate near the larch plantation and forward to intercept a descending track to retrace your steps to Millthrop. When you meet the village road turn right and take the first road on the left to go down to a T-junction near the Rawthey bridge. Over the bridge follow the lane back into Sedbergh.

# 31 Dent and Barbondale

*This fine walk begins with an easy amble along a stretch of the Dales Way before launching itself up the hillside above in order to visit a couple of old farmsteads and cross into the entrance to Barbondale. A final flourish takes the route along an ancient track, the Occupation Road, which linked Ingleton and Lancaster. The road also marked the upper reaches of the 'occupied' land below during the 19th century.*

| | |
|---|---|
| **Distance:** 5½ miles/9km | walking on clear paths and |
| **Height gain:** 820ft/250m | ancient tracks |
| **Walking time:** 3 hours | **Start/Finish:** Dent |
| **Type of walk:** Good | GR704871 |

From the Dent car park turn right and walk along the road for about 400yds/m, taking care against approaching traffic in the absence of a footpath.

Just after the road from Dent and the River Dee run side by side, leave the road, on the right, over a low stile onto a footpath signposted to Barth Bridge. The path runs on alongside the river on an obvious green path across fields until it reaches the bridge.

Cross the bridge and follow the road for a little over 400yds/m. Just before leaving the road you pass the memorial to Lucy Elam mentioned in

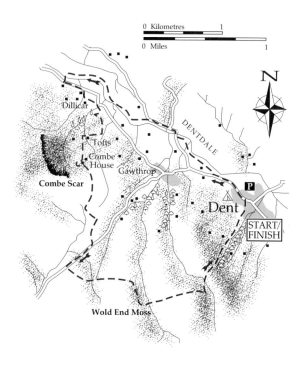

Walk 30. Having passed this, leave the road, at a bend, by going left at a footpath (signposted: Mire House) which passes through a small stand of beech and sycamore to a stile. Beyond you drop towards the river, and can go forward along flood embankments. The path is never far from the river, crossing a number of fields, and eventually leading to a footbridge at Ellers.

Over the footbridge, turn left along the road for

200yds/m to a ladder stile on the right. Over this go up the ensuing field (trackless) for about 100yds/m and then cross to a hedgerow gap on the left to go into Dillicar Farm. As you enter the farmyard, bear left to locate and follow its access.

When you reach a road junction, keep forward for 40yds/m and then turn right at a signposted footpath to Bower Bank and Stone Rigg. The path immediately zigzags left and right to climb as a vehicle track across a sloping pasture. The track peters out near a ruined farm building. Go forward to the left of the building, and having passed it, keep on up to the top corner of the pasture.

*Across the valley below is the whaleback ridge of Aye Gill Pike, while looking to the north, the rounded, pale summits of the Howgills peer over the intervening ridge of Helms Knott. More impressively, the great gritstone screes of Combe Scar loom above the route, and resound to the call of buzzard and the occasional raven.*

Through a gate you step onto a broad track. Turn right on this and walk on to derelict Tofts Farm. Go between the farmyard buildings and through a gate, descending right and left to cross a stream. Climb left on the other side on a narrow path until you meet a rough track. Turn right along this to go through a wall gap, and follow the rising green track beyond. This climbs to Combe House Farm, another derelict building, sheltering below the craggy slopes of Combe Scar in a truly splendid setting. Go to the right of the farm buildings and continue just above a derelict wall to head out on a terraced green track that would have been the farm's access, contouring across the hillside.

*As you march out onto the moorland slopes, Dent suddenly appears in the valley below, perfectly set above the river. Further on, the valley head is closed by the squat mound of Great Knoutberry Hill on the slopes of which you can sometimes pick out the trains on the Settle to Carlisle railway line.*

Gradually as you swing round to face the austere moorland slopes of Barbondale, the route bears left as a green track, and then cuts right to cross a patch of marshy ground to a ladder stile. Over this, bear right on an initially indistinct grassy path, that passes through the moderately hummocky terrain of Stone Rigg, eventually to find its way over to a wall corner and a gate by which you reach the Barbondale road.

Turn right along the road for about 400yds/m, and then leave it by turning left onto a broad walled stony track, the Occupation Road, signposted to Dent, Nun House and High Moss. Follow this old highway as it crosses South Lord's Land for about 1¼ miles (2.2km) until you can branch left onto a signposted bridleway going down through a gate and Flinters Gill beyond to Dent.

When you reach a surfaced lane follow it forward between cottages to reach the village green, and keep on in the same direction to the main village road.

# 32 The Calf

*It is Cautley, Calf and Winder that, according to a
Sedbergh School Song, "makes the Sedbergh man", and it
is by these three features, and more, that this high level
walk goes. If time is short, you can simply return from
The Calf, but here a longer finish is suggested that will
take you into remote Bowderdale and down to visit
Cautley Spout, an often spectacular waterfall.*

**Distance:** *10½ miles/17km*
**Height gain:** *2,050ft
/625m*
**Walking time:** *5-6 hours*
**Type of walk:** *In spite of
easy going underfoot this*
*is a strenuous walk.
Not recommended in
poor visibility.*
**Start/Finish:** *Loftus Hill
Car Park, Sedbergh.
GR658919*

The walk begins from the Loftus Hill Car Park from
where you go up past the church to the main
street. Turn left for a short distance, and then right
along a minor road (signposted: Howgill),
following this as it ascends to the road up to
Lockbank Farm. Go through the farm and onto the
open fellside, climbing steeply up a slanting green
rake that leads up and across the lower slopes of
Winder (the 'i' pronounced as in 'win'), and soon
changes from a north-west direction to north-east.

At this point divert to take in Winder, either by

tackling the slope ahead straight on, or by going left, still climbing until an easier gradient is reached, and then heading east to the summit. From the top, a good path leads north-east to rejoin the original path at a small cairn. Continue easily to an unmarked grassy path heading north to the summit of Arant Haw.

As with Winder, a good path heads north-east from the summit of Arant Haw to rejoin the main path at a small collapsed cairn. The path drops to cross Rowantree Grains, as a fence appears on the right. This fence will guide you to within a few paces of the summit of Calders, though the path is clear enough. Nearing the top of Calders the path bends sharply, and passes close by the summit cairn.

In poor visibility, take care not to continue along the path beside the fence; this doesn't take you to The Calf. If necessary, a compass bearing will put you on the right line and soon lead you onto the right path for the highest of these fine fells.

The quickest way back to Sedbergh is to return by the onward route just described, and if time is short this is the best option. Otherwise locate and follow a path, running north-east to a small tarn (sometimes dried up), where the path forks. The left branch takes you down over Hazelgill Knott to Bowderdale village, but follow instead the right fork. It, too, leads into Bowderdale, this time into the valley of that name.

The watershed in Bowderdale marks the boundary

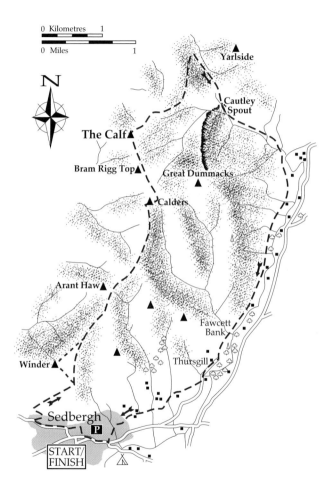

0 Kilometres 1

0 Miles 1

N

▲ Yarlside

Cautley
Spout

The Calf ▲

Bram Rigg Top ▲

Great Dummacks
▲

▲ Calders

Arant Haw ▲

▲

▲

Fawcett
Bank

▲

Thursgill

Winder ▲

Sedbergh
P

START/
FINISH

of the national park, and this broad, flat col is your objective. By staying on the path descending from The Calf, you needlessly go too far north into Bowderdale. Instead, when you feel you can cope with the untracked ground on the right, descend across it to reach the valley bottom near a makeshift sheepfold. Cross the stream, and follow a narrow path leading south to the steep descent east of Cautley Spout. In good conditions you will have fine views of this magnificent fall, which may be approached more closely by ascending the prominent Cautley Spout Tongue.

Down into the broad valley of Cautley Holme Beck, the path heads for the prominent temperance inn, the Cross Keys, but as you reach the valley bottom, leave this and bear right (south) to cross the beck by a footbridge. At a subsequent barn, take the right fork and ascend slightly behind it to follow a good path leading to a gate in the intake wall.

The path continues easily through fields, passing a number of gates and stiles until Fawcett Bank farm is reached, at the entrance to Hobdale. Here the track improves dramatically, and leads across Hobdale Beck by a bridge (gate), and on to Thursgill, Ellerthwaite and Buckbank, by a delightful and now motorable road to reach the A683 a mile (1.5km) from the starting point. Turn right to return to Sedbergh.

# 33 The Eastern Howgills

*The first half of this circular walk in classic Howgill country contains most of the hard work, while the rest by comparison is gentle. These delectable eastern fells receive far less attention than the rest, and are more likely to provide you with a quiet day.*

**Distance:** *9 miles/15km*
**Height gain:** *3,310ft/1,010m*
**Walking time:** *5-6 hours*
**Type of walk:** *An energetic walk with a lot of up and down and some steep slopes*
**Start/Finish:** *The Cross Keys Inn: parking alongside road, near footbridge. GR698969*

*Set aside from the fells of Lakeland and the familiar heights of the Dales, the Howgills form a unique, virtually untramped wilderness of considerable charm and beauty. In most lights, and especially from afar, they have a translucent, almost seductive sheen, completely lacking in sharp edges: soft, flowing hills that spread themselves luxuriously between the Lune and the Rawthey.*

*Unlike the fells west across Bowderdale, the summits tackled on this walk are not connected by high ground, and so call for a fair amount of descent and re-ascent. But don't let that deter you, for all the real effort comes*

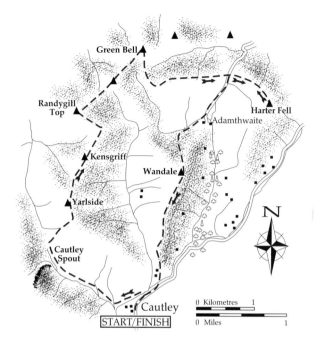

at the start of the walk.

*The circuit begins at the Cross Keys Temperance Hotel on the Sedbergh-Kirkby Stephen road, a National Trust property, described as: "A small whitewashed inn, built circa 1600 and altered in the early eighteenth and late nineteenth centuries. Acquired in 1949 with 17 acres of land, under the Will of Mrs E. A. Bunney, to be held as an unlicensed inn in memory of her sister Miss M. B. Hewetson."*

Near the hotel a footbridge crosses the River Rawthey. Over it bear left on a good path into a pleasant flat-bottomed valley. Ahead, the falls of Cautley Spout are prominent against the broken cliffs of Cautley Crag, the only significant expanse of rock in the Howgills. The way now lies up a steeply ascending path far to the right of the falls by which you reach the broad col of Bowderdale Head.

If you have the time it is worth diverting to clamber up Cautley Spout Tongue to gain a better view of the falls. The falls are among the highest in the country, having a vertical height of more than 700ft/200m. When you near the top of the falls you can safely cross right (north) and so gain Bowderdale Head.

Bowderdale Beck finds its source high on the southern slopes of Yarlside, and you now follow it to ascend trackless ground to the shallow col south of the summit. Once at the col it is an easy matter to ascend to the summit.

*The view from Yarlside is quite remarkable in spite of the restriction south-west which the slightly higher ground of The Calf plateau imposes. The Lakeland fells spread across the distant skyline from the Coniston massif to the fells of Mungrisdale. The highest summits of the Pennines, Cross Fell and the Dun Fells, rise high above the Eden valley, while nearer at hand, Wild Boar Fell, Swarth Fell and Baugh Fell frame a cameo of the Wensleydale hills. The panorama is completed by the unmistakable summits of Whernside, Ingleborough and Pen-y-ghent.*

The continuation to the minor intermediate summit, Kensgriff, involves the descent of a very steep grassy slope to the Saddle, demanding great care especially in icy conditions. Beyond Kensgriff all that lost height has to be regained on the ascent, easy but steep, to the top of Randygill Top.

*These two summits must be the most impressive of all the Howgills, and it is from here that the appeal of the range will most impress itself. If you've reached this far, you will be relieved to know that the hard part is now over.*

North-east now a faint path leads down to and over a minor bump, Stockless, before rising gently to the trig on Green Bell. This northerly summit looks down on the Lune valley, towards Weasdale and Newbiggin. Only a short distance down its north-east slope a few bubbling springs well up, the birthplace of the Lune, and worth a quick diversion.

By retreating slightly, south from Green Bell, you cross pathless ground over Grere Fell and Adamthwaite Bank, tackling a few boggy passages on the way to the minor road linking the farm at Adamthwaite with Ravenstonedale. It is only a short excursion across the road to visit the summit of Harter Fell and to return to the road.

Having regained the road turn left until a distinct green track branches right near a small plantation, passing the farm at Adamthwaite. Lying south of the watershed, Adamthwaite nevertheless is served by an access road from Ravenstonedale, over the hill to the north. This is a delightful spot, deep set among trees, remote, unsuspected and rarely visited by walkers.

Continue through a gate in a crosswall, and on past a barn to another gate in the wall on the left. From here it is a gentle climb to the top of Wandale Fell, followed by an equally easy descent south-west to a path dropping down to Narthwaite, a cluster of buildings perched on the crest of a hill. A footbridge spans Backside Beck, and by using the bridleway it carries an easy return to the Rawthey footbridge.

# 34 Carlin Gill

*This walk is an exciting route plunging deep into the folds of the western Howgills. After prolonged wet weather some parts of the route are potentially difficult, but otherwise the walk is among the highlights of the whole range. To complete a satisfying circuit, above Carlin Gill the walk takes in some of the lower fells flanking the Lune gorge.*

**Distance:** *7¹/₂ miles/12km*
**Height gain:** *1,510ft/460m*
**Walking time:** *4-5 hours*
**Type of walk:** *Scrambly and moorland walking*
**Start/Finish:** *Salterwath Bridge: parking for one or two cars. GR612009*

*Carlin Gill is one of the not-quite-so-hidden secrets of the Howgills — it's plainly obvious from the M6 motorway — a splendid thrust into the soft flesh of the fells at a point where a number of streams gather to form splendid waterfalls. The route begins along the boundary of the Yorkshire Dales National Park, and though very little is on rights of way, the whole route has been walked for many years and considerate walkers are unlikely to be troubled. Because so much of the second part of the route is across trackless moorland fell tops, it is inadvisable to think of doing this walk in poor visibility.*

The walk begins at Salterwath Bridge, on an old

packhorse route, near Low Borrow Bridge, where the Romans positioned a fort. There used to be an inn here, too, the meeting place of the local manorial court.

The road from Salterwath, once the Roman road, leads easily to Carlin Gill bridge. Here you gain access to the true right bank of Carlingill Beck, to be followed until Weasel Gill descends to join it from the slopes of Uldale Head. Now cross the beck to reach a sheep track on the opposite bank that leads into a quite different world.

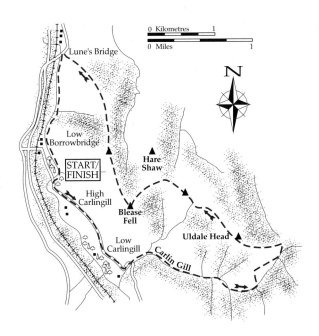

Ahead the gill cuts sharply into the fellsides, creating a steep-sided ravine with a bed so narrow that progress is only possible by hopping from bank to bank, grappling with fallen trees, and balancing on boulders that in times of spate are well and truly submerged.

Within minutes you move from gentle grazing lands to wild and chaotic scenery, that could be miles from anywhere. Remorselessly, the gill closes in, groups of birch and alder cling to the banks, forcing you to dodge and weave about to make progress. Suddenly a broad gash opens up on the right as you reach the foot of Black Force, a rocky gorge of considerable severity in otherwise gentle surroundings, down which plunges a series of waterfalls.

Beyond the entrance to Black Force, after more dancing with the beck, you are faced by yet another waterfall, The Spout, one that efficiently restricts forward progress. Two escapes present themselves. The simplest is to tackle the very steep grassy fellside on the right (south), to reach a horizontal path which will lead you left into the upper reaches of the gill. Alternatively, climb the narrow rib which contains The Spout in a small amphitheatre. A sequence of footsteps takes you up to meet a slabby section of friable rock, which must be crossed with care before the security of firmer ground above is reached.

Once above The Spout you continue by following the beck until finally you emerge on a broad grassy plateau, Blakethwaite Bottom, in the middle of which stands an isolated boulder, Blakethwaite Stone. This once marked the boundary between Yorkshire and the now defunct county of Westmorland.

From Blakethwaite Bottom ascend west up the grassy slopes of Uldale Head to a large cairn before pressing on a short way further to its summit. What follows is a purely delightful stroll across Howgill fells. Largely trackless, though paths come and go, the going is nowhere difficult.

Your immediate objective is the flat col north-east of Blease Fell, between the heads of Ellergill Beck and Grains Gills. From here a short ascent takes you to the top of Blease Fell. By descending the broad north ridge of Blease Fell to a shallow col due east of Lune's Bridge you can then descend to a disused quarry (GR614030) to meet the old turnpike road.

A few minutes south along the road brings us to the access road to Brockholes Farm. Follow this to the farm, and keep ahead on entering the farmyard. The map shows a right of way passing north of the farm buildings, but I have never been able to get through this way, and the farmer has directed me through the farmyard, immediately then to turn right to head for the banks of the Lune.

All that now remains is a pleasant amble alongside the river, until a path through a final section of woodland brings you abruptly back to Salterwath Bridge.

# 35 The Fairmile Round

*Entriangled by the Lune gorge to the west, the headwaters of the River Lune to the north and the Rathey valley to the east, the "naked heights" of the Howgills, to quote Wordsworth, are a splendid composition of steep-flanked, bald-pated fells of outstanding and simple beauty. In this circular tour, you visit the highest summit, and include a number of other worthy tops, too, before romping home above the valley intake wall.*

| | |
|---|---|
| **Distance:** 8¹/₂ miles /13.5km | *easy, over undulating, broad summits that are confusing in mist* |
| **Height gain:** 2,640ft /805m | **Start/Finish:** *Just north of* |
| **Walking time:** 4-5 hours | *Fairmile Gate.* |
| **Type of walk:** *Generally* | *GR629982* |

*The Fairmile Round, as I have called this circuit, is an unashamed attempt to get, at one go, the most pleasure possible from a western approach to the summits. It begins, just north of Fairmile Gate, from open pastureland flanking the minor road that follows the line of the Roman road through the Lune valley to the site of the fort at Low Borrowbridge.*

Start by following the obvious grassy path that roughly and steeply follows the line of Dry Gill until, as the gradient eases, you can move right to gain the top of Linghaw, an excellent vantage point that embraces Pennine, Dales and Lakeland summits as well as a view of Morecambe Bay.

Head south-eastwards on a faint path descending to a grassy col crossed by a path rising from Beck Houses. Cross the col and climb again to Fell Head's subsidiary summit, before climbing to the main top.

The continuing route now curves around the head of Long Rigg Beck, where a collection of feeder streams share the name Crooked Ashmere Gills, before descending steeply to a neat col, Windscarth Wyke. From there ascend steadily to a minor top, Bush Howe, from where a good path, initially descending, makes for the distant, prominent trig pillar on The Calf, the highest summit of the Howgills.

From The Calf a broad path presses on east of south, making for Calders, passing on the way a minor, grassy summit, Bram Rigg Top. You'll need to divert to include Bram Rigg Top in the walk, but, if you descend a little down its west-facing slopes, it has the advantage of being a fine and lofty place to take a break and enjoy the view of the low-lying eastern and southern fells of the Lakeland fringe.

From Calders another diversion is possible, a digression north of east to reach the top of Cautley Crags, which spill from an otherwise uninteresting summit known as Great Dummacks. To continue from Calders, parallel a fenceline first heading in a south-westwards direction and then south on a

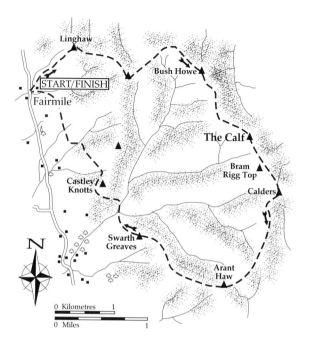

broad track as it descends steeply to a narrow col. This track ultimately presses on over the tops to Winder and the village of Sedbergh, but leave it behind just after the col and aim instead for the top of Arant Haw, a fine summit at the head of Crosdale Beck.

Leaving Arant Haw's top, descend its long western ridge, gradually bearing north-west to reach the confluence between Bram Rigg Beck and Chapel Beck, which lies beneath the minor hump of

Castley Knotts. You may have to divert upstream to cross with dry feet — though there are times, too, when you may have to settle for wet feet.

Your on-going objective now is to follow the intake wall across trackless countryside that lies below Castley Knotts, Brown Moor and Whin's End, finally crossing Fairmile Beck to return to your starting point.

# Other Dalesman titles for walkers

### Walking and Trail Guides
*Lake District Western Fells* Paddy Dillon £4.99
*Lake District Eastern Fells* Paddy Dillon £4.99
*Yorkshire Dales North & East* Terry Marsh £4.99

### Walks Around Series: Yorkshire
*Grassington* Richard Musgrave £1.99
*Hawes* Richard Musgrave £1.99
*Helmsley* Nick Channer £1.99
*Kirkbymoorside* Nick Channer £1.99
*Pickering* Nick Channer £1.99
*Richmond* Richard Musgrave £1.99
*Settle & Malham* Richard Musgrave £1.99
*Whitby* Nick Channer £1.99

### Walks Around Series: Lake District
*Ambleside* Tom Bowker £1.99
*Coniston & Hawkshead* Mary Welsh £1.99
*Keswick* Dawn Gibson £1.99
*Windermere* Robert Gambles £1.99

### Pub Walks Series
*Lancashire* Terry Marsh £5.99
*Lake District* Terry Marsh £5.99
*North York Moors & Coast* Richard Musgrave £5.99

### Tea Shop Walks Series
*Lake District* Mary Welsh £5.99
*Peak District* Andrew McCloy £5.99
*Yorkshire Dales* Richard Musgrave £5.99
*North York Moors & Coast* Mark Reid £5.99

***Walker's Guide Series***
*Three Peaks & Malhamdale* W R Mitchell £6.95
*Cleveland Hills* Tom Scott Burns £6.95

***Long-Distance Walks***
*Cumbria Way* John Trevelyan £2.99
*Dales Way* Colin Speakman £2.99

***Safety for Walkers***
*Map Reading* Robert Matkin £3.50

Available from all good bookshops.
In case of difficulty, or for a full list of
Dalesman titles, contact:
Dalesman Publishing
The Water Mill, Broughton Hall,
Skipton, North Yorkshire BD23 3AG.
*Tel:* (+44) 01756 701033
*Website:* www.dalesman.co.uk